Andrea M'Laughlin & Robin Hanover Nov 97

D1140404

The
ALEXANDER
TECHNIQUE
For Pregnancy
And Childbirth

Brita Forsstrom is an Alexander teacher and a mother. She first trained in librarianship and followed this with a short spell working as a journalist in her native Sweden. She has run a private practice since 1984 and regularly gives workshops and talks. She is also experienced in teaching groups of pregnant women and new mothers. Brita Forsstrom lives in Bloomsbury, London.

Mel Hampson has a degree in psychology, and has worked as an editor and copywriter in this area. She is a trained midwife and has a private practice teaching the Alexander Technique, regularly running introductory courses and working with pregnant women both individually and in antenatal Alexander groups. She is currently studying for a Masters degree in Occupational Psychology. Mel Hampson lives in Hampstead, London.

Nancy Durrell McKenna is an award-winning photographer and film maker specializing in pregnancy and childbirth and Third World issues.

THE
ALEXANDER
TECHNIQUE
FOR PREGNANCY
AND CHILDBIRTH

BRITA FORSSTROM AND MEL HAMPSON

Photographs by Nancy Durrell McKenna

VICTOR GOLLANCZ
LONDON

First published in Great Britain 1995 by Victor Gollancz
A Division of the Cassell group
Wellington House, 125–130 Strand, London WC2R 0BB

A Gollancz Paperback Original © Brita Forsstrom and Mel Hampson 1995

All rights reserved. No part of this publication may be reproduced or transmitted in
any form or by any means, electronic or mechanical including photocopying,
recording or any information storage or retrieval system, without prior permission
in writing from the publishers.

The right of Brita Forsstrom and Mel Hampson to be identified as authors of this
work has been asserted by them in accordance with the Copyright, Designs and
Patents Act, 1988.

A catalogue record for this book is available from the British Library.

ISBN 0 575 05486 7

Designed by Robert Updegraff
Line illustrations by Karen Hiscock
Printed by The Bath Press, Avon

CONTENTS

Introduction   *7*

PART ONE: What Is the Alexander Technique?   9
1   Alexander Technique: the Theory   10
2   The Alexander Technique in Practice   33

PART TWO: The Alexander Way for Pregnancy   52
3   Use in Pregnancy   54
4   Everyday Activities During Pregnancy   67
5   Breathing in Pregnancy   74
6   Common Complaints in Pregnancy   82

PART THREE: Labour and Birth   88
7   Use in Labour   89
8   The Process of Labour   107
9   Overcoming Fear and Pain in Labour   120
10 Birth Support   128

PART FOUR: The Alexander Technique for Parenting   131
11 After the Baby Is Born   131
12 Looking After Your Baby with Good Use   138
13 Use and Your Child   152

Further Reading   *157*
Useful Addresses   *157*
Index   *159*

Brita: For Ann-Mari, my mother, and Anna, my daughter

Mel: For Jackie, my mother

We shall not cease from exploration
And the end of all our exploring
Will be to arrive where we started
And know the place for the first time.
Little Gidding, T. S. Eliot

Acknowledgements

Brita: I wish to thank the following who have helped to see the book through from conception to birth: Veronica Peck for passing it my way, all the pregnant women and new mothers whom I have taught, and who have been a great source of inspiration, John Nicholls for support in my own learning process, Sam McCarter for seeing me through a sticky patch, Susan Fleming for her editing and many friends and colleagues for providing comments, suggestions and encouragement, and and finally a special thanks to John and Anna for their loving support during the time of writing.

Mel: I'd like to thank all the women I have had the pleasure of working with and of learning from during their childbearing year; and my friends and colleagues for generously contributing their ideas to this book. My heartfelt thanks go to all my friends for their love and support, most especially Heather Amos, Jenny Ashworth, Susan Dailey, Mark Gessler, and my partner Simon Wilkinson.

We would both like to express our thanks to the following: Sean Carey, Jean Clark, Claire Dannatt, Helen Gibson (Johnson), Sheila Gleeson, Judy Hammond, Christine Matheson, Lynne Nicholls, Jenny Norton, Janet Pinder, Refia Sacks, Liz Scannell, Monique Stone and Francoise Urquhart for their wealth of contributions; Nancy Durrell-McKenna for the photography, Robert Updegraff for the design, Karen Hiscock for her splendid illustrations, Roz Lewis for her editing skills, and Katrina Whone at Victor Gollancz for her continual optimism and patience in seeing the book through to production.

INTRODUCTION

Mel: the midwife's perspective

While practising as a midwife I was privileged to share in the joy of many women's pregnancy, birthing and early days with the baby. However, I was saddened to see a widespread acceptance of the common complaints of pregnancy and also of the frequency with which medical intervention was used for the birth.

Although I believed that the approach taken by the medical profession was partly to blame, I also felt there were other factors: a large majority of women lead busy and stressful lives, which precludes adequate time for exercise and relaxation; and the prevailing cultural belief in Britain is that birth is painful and dangerous. I felt strongly that, in addition to changes in hospital practices, women themselves needed to take some practical steps to promote a healthy pregnancy, and also to regain confidence in their own ability to give birth.

I reluctantly stopped working as a midwife because of a debilitating back problem. My training in the Alexander Technique not only gave me a strong back, but a new and satisfying way to work with pregnant women, addressing the problems I had encountered as a midwife. The understanding of the intimate relationship between mind and body that is learned in the Technique effects the most fundamental changes in a woman's approach to childbearing and motherhood.

I have found that the Technique facilitates a more comfortable and enjoyable pregnancy, engenders a trust that birth is a normal physiological process and prepares a woman for actively participating in the birth of her baby. It gives her the skills for looking after herself while caring for the newborn child, and maintaining a healthy sense of her own self at this time when the boundaries between mother and child become so blurred.

Of course, practising the Alexander Technique does not mean there will be no difficulties, but it does give women the ability to have real choice and control, whatever the circumstances. Thus, for all women, childbirth can be a positive and enriching experience, laying strong foundations for parenthood.

Mel Hampson, London, November 1994

Brita: the mother's perspective

Pregnancy is the start of a journey into the unknown. Although we can find out a great deal about what to expect from pregnancy, childbirth and parenthood, our own experiences will be new and our reactions unpredictable. When I was pregnant I often felt that books, midwives and doctors were concerned with the pregnancy independently of me, with much emphasis on the end result, the baby. I sometimes wondered 'What about me, what about afterwards?' For me the Alexander Technique provided the missing link.

This very practical method teaches us a better way to 'use' ourselves – mind and body – and thus promotes healthy functioning in general, and hence of the processes of pregnancy and birth. Its main concern is with teaching us to have choice and control over our reactions as a means to establish this better 'use', and it was this aspect of the Technique that I found most helpful. It helped me to keep a sense of myself and yet to allow the constant changes in my body and lifestyle. I was able to go on teaching right up to six days before going into labour. I also had the benefit of having Diana Aubrey, friend and Alexander teacher, with me in the labour ward. Her 'hands-on direction' during the pushing stage helped enormously. The Technique was invaluable in the recovery afterwards, and as the years of motherhood pass by (often too quickly!) I continue to receive constant help and inspiration from the work.

I hope the reader too will be inspired to learn and benefit from it, as I believe that the Alexander Technique is the ideal preparation for pregnancy, birth, parenthood, and beyond.

Brita Forsstrom, London, November 1994

PART ONE
What Is the Alexander Technique?

The Alexander Technique is a form of sensory re-education that teaches people how to eliminate ingrained habits of body 'misuse' and stress patterns, commonly experienced as physical disorders such as bad backs, neck problems and headaches, or mental and emotional problems such as irritability or depression.

The Technique was discovered over a hundred years ago, and has been taught in this country for many years. People approach the Technique for a variety of reasons. Some have heard it will help the aforementioned conditions, some are simply attracted to the ideas that underpin the work. Whatever the reason, pupils of the Technique all have one thing in common – they want to change and improve conditions that stop them enjoying a happy, healthy life.

Although primarily a physical teaching (teachers gently use their hands to help change the body) the Technique has important philosophical concepts behind it, which makes it more than a simple therapy. It is not a passive treatment, such as osteopathy or massage, with which it is often erroneously compared. The difference lies in the teacher's approach to the pupil and their problems. The Technique leans on its philosophical background and encourages the pupil to *think*, to become more conscious, to learn awareness of the mind and body in order to heal themselves.

In this book we will be showing how the Alexander Technique can be helpful during pregnancy and childbirth, and in caring for babies and small children. We strongly recommend that you use this book as an adjunct to direct experience of having lessons yourself, as no amount of text can hope to convey the personal experience that will be unique to you and your body when you start to practise Alexander work. First, though, let us look at the basic principles of the Technique, and explain some of the terms Alexander coined to describe his work.

1 Alexander Technique: the Theory

F.M. Alexander and His Discovery

The Alexander Technique takes its name from an Australian actor, Frederick Matthias Alexander (1869–1955), who, as a result of solving his own vocal problem, made some far-reaching discoveries about human behaviour and general health and well-being.

His promising career as an actor was first clouded and then threatened by persistent throat problems, which frequently led to a temporary loss of voice. Doctors could do nothing to help him, so in desperation and frustration he decided to take matters into his own hands.

As the vocal problem was brought on by reciting, Alexander decided to observe himself in a mirror to see if he could find out what he did to cause it. Over months and later years, Alexander's painstaking examination of his own posture revealed that he stiffened his neck muscles, pulled his head back and down and audibly gasped every time he spoke. On further observation he noticed that this way of using his voice was part of a muscular tension pattern which included how he used his whole body. The pattern was in fact present in everything he did and involved a disturbance of the intricate poise and flexible balance of his head, neck and back. He discovered that changing the way he used these parts was the key to improving the general use of his body.

Having found that this pattern occurred at the moment he got ready to recite, he had to *stop* himself before he began reciting, so he could then proceed to find a new and better way of using his head, neck and back when speaking. In this way he was able to gradually change his *habitual* use of himself.

Free from the old habits associated with the use of his voice, Alexander's breathing difficulties disappeared, excess tension was released, and he experienced greater freedom of movement, as well as improved health and well-being. His reputation as an actor grew as he became famous for the splendid control of his voice and graceful presence on stage, and having so successfully solved his own problem, colleagues and people who came to hear him recite wanted to know how he had done it. Before long, teaching his new technique had taken over from acting as his main occupation in life.

In 1904 Alexander came to London where he soon built up a flourishing practice. He was especially popular with people from the theatre, among them Sir Henry Irving, Herbert Beerbohm Tree and Lily Langtry. Many other famous people came to Alexander for lessons and have written about his work. These include George Bernard Shaw, Sir Stafford Cripps and Aldous Huxley. The American philosopher John Dewey (sometimes called the 'father of the American education system') learned of Alexander's work and became a great proponent of the Technique. When Professor Nikolaas Tinbergen received the 1973 Nobel prize for Physiology and Medicine, he devoted half his speech to the Alexander Technique.

In 1931 Alexander started to train others to teach his Technique, working with his hands and referring to the books he had written in order to impart the essence of his very personal gifts. He died in 1955, teaching right up to the week before his death, still as dedicated to his work as ever. His tradition lives on through those he taught, and there are now teachers in many countries worldwide, the greatest concentration being in England and America.

Mind and Body

Before he began his many years of self-investigation, Alexander held the common view of his time that the body and the mind were separate, and that any illnesses and difficulties should be classified as either 'mental' or 'physical'. However, his practical experience in solving his voice problem made Alexander look at the role of his mind in what he was doing. He came to the opinion that any activity, whether it is 'lifting an arm, or walking, talking, going to sleep, starting out to learn something, thinking out a problem, or making a decision', involves an interrelationship between both 'mental' and 'physical' processes, and that it is impossible to separate activities into either purely mental or purely physical.

This indivisible unity of the mind and body he called 'psycho-physical unity', and it is one of the fundamental principles of the Alexander Technique. We are probably aware of this in our everyday lives. For example, most of us are all too familiar with the way anxiety can affect us. We can have difficulty breathing, feel nauseous and notice our movements become stiff and jerky. Or when trying to solve a complicated mathematical problem in our heads, we frown with concentration and hold our breath. Equally, when we have been physically inactive for a while – maybe writing a difficult letter – and we go for a walk or a swim, not only do we think more clearly, but we feel a lot better.

Use of the Self

Alexander teachers talk about how we 'use ourselves', and on first hearing, this expression may seem strange. Although we talk about using a tool or an instrument for a specific purpose, we do not normally talk about how we use ourselves, except when we say things like 'Use your head!'. Alexander did talk about 'using oneself' in the sense of using a piece of equipment, but he did not mean it in the limited and mechanical sense of how we use a specific part of the body, such as an arm or a leg. He meant it in a wider sense that encompassed the way we use the whole of the human organism – including the way in which we think and feel. It is the way we use ourselves in everything we do – the way we breathe, talk, eat, walk, sit and stand up. It is the way we live our lives, our very approach to life, and it goes on *constantly*, for better or for worse.

Use Affects Functioning

Alexander's initial discovery, that when he was reciting he pulled his head back strongly and that this was causing hoarseness, was to have far-reaching implications. Naturally, when he corrected this tendency his voice improved, but that was not all. He was rewarded with an improvement of his general functioning. He felt better within himself, he breathed much more easily and movement was altogether much freer. He concluded that it was the *use* of himself that determined whether he functioned well or badly, and from this observation he established the principle that 'use affects functioning'. (It is important to remember that 'functioning' encompasses the person as a whole, which is the way we function mentally and emotionally as well as physically.)

That 'use affects functioning' is something we all know intuitively from our everyday lives. For example, if we drive a car with the handbrake on (i.e. with misuse), first of all it will not go so fast, and second the brakes will be damaged (i.e. its functioning will be impaired). Although the analogy is not quite accurate because human beings are far more sophisticated than machines, it still holds true that poor or faulty use – or misuse – is bound to cause poor functioning.

Alexander's radical idea, then, is that the way we use ourselves will influence a whole range of functional problems such as tension headaches, breathing and circulatory disorders, backache, sleeping problems, general stress and wear and tear on joints. Of course, there are many other causes of illness and poor functioning – Alexander did not claim that he had a miracle cure – such as hereditary and environmental factors, trauma and injury. Yet the unique thing about use is that it is a factor over which we can have control. We are the person who operates the equipment: we 'use' ourselves.

In keeping with Alexander's philosophical point that it is the whole body that needs improving upon, a teacher will always encourage an overall improvement of use over and above focusing on specific symptoms. The idea is that if poor use is the cause of a problem, then improving general use often helps the specific problem that the pupil has. Even if poor use is not the direct cause of the problem, improved use, which has a beneficial effect on all our body systems, will often aid recovery.

Primary Control or Head/Neck/Back Relationship

The 'use' of himself that Alexander realized was causing a poor functioning was the way he over-contracted his neck muscles and pulled his head backwards and downwards into his shoulders. This had the effect of compressing his spine, causing a shortening and narrowing of the whole of the torso, and stiffening of all the muscles throughout his body. When he shortened his stature in this way his voice became hoarse.

He found that when he was able to prevent himself from stiffening his neck and pulling his head back and down, and allowed his head to go in a forwards and upwards direction in relation to the spine, this released the compression of the spine. As a result, his torso lengthened and widened and furthermore there was a lessening of muscular tension throughout his whole body. With this lengthening of his stature his voice improved.

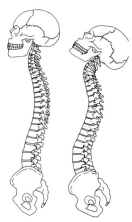

When the head goes forward and up, the spine is allowed to lengthen. When the head is pulled back, the spine becomes excessively curved and shortened.

From these observations, Alexander realized that it was the relationship between the parts of the central axis of the body, that is, between the head and the neck, and the head and neck in relation to the rest of the back, which determined his overall use and functioning. This led him to the discovery that the head, neck and back relationship constituted an inbuilt mechanism for organizing or controlling upright posture, movement and co-ordination throughout the whole body. Alexander called this the 'primary control', and according to him it is the key to developing our awareness and good use in all our activities.

When people first have Alexander lessons they often try to put their head in a certain position, and ask their teacher if 'this is "it"'. Unfortunately for us, the primary control is not a static position of the head on the spine, a 'magic' position to be found and then held, but rather when the head is poised and freely movable, the spine is well aligned and is working as a smoothly functioning whole. The primary control is basically a dynamic relationship between the head, neck and back, an attitude, if you like, and the only definite way of understanding it is to have an Alexander teacher show you what it is and then experience the postural changes that come about.

LEFT: *Maintaining a good head/neck/ back relationship in movement.*

RIGHT: *Pulling the head back and shortening the back.*

 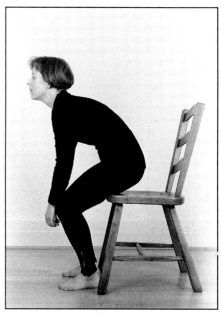

With this dynamic relationship of the head neck and back, the head is free to initiate movement. All vertebrates (this includes us!) are designed so that it is the movement of the head that leads the movement of the rest of the body. You can see this mechanism working superbly when a cat spots its prey. It is very clearly the head that goes first and the spine follows, and its four limbs move the body in the direction the head is dictating. This is harder to appreciate in human beings where we have effectively come up on to our hind legs and have two directions to deal with – our spines go upwards while we move forwards. However, we still work best, like other animals, when the head is leading and the spine is following – and this is what occurs when we have a good head/neck/back relationship.

We can see the primary control working well in happy healthy children, animals, people in so-called 'primitive' cultures and some athletes. There is an observable poise in the posture and an ease and lightness in the quality of movement. It is also noticeable that there is an increased co-ordination between the parts of the body: most importantly, the movements of the arms and the legs are dictated by the movement of the head, neck and back, rather than the other way round.

In the text of the book, for ease of understanding, we have sometimes used the term primary control and sometimes the head/neck/back relationship.

'The primary control is there for anyone who cares to come along and use it.'
F.M. Alexander

More on the Physiology of the Primary Control

If we take a closer look at the physiology of the head/neck interaction we can see why this relationship is so important. The head weighs approximately 4–6 kilograms, a considerable weight to carry around on top of the spine. (Fortunately for us, we do not experience it as being so heavy.) It is balanced on the top vertebra of the spine at a joint called the atlanto-occipital joint. Because it is heavier in front of its pivot point, there is a constant tendency for the head to fall forwards. This is prevented by the co-ordinated action of the neck muscles, and is why, when someone falls asleep sitting upright and their neck muscles relax their head falls forwards.

There are two muscle groups at the back of the neck that are involved in the balance of the head on the body. An inner layer consists of smaller muscles – the sub-occipital muscles – and their job is to make the continual subtle adjustments necessary to maintain the delicate and freely moving balance of the head on the spine.

Unfortunately, in the majority of people the subtle balancing act of the head on top of the spine is not allowed to function, because the larger, outer layer of neck muscles, which run between the head and upper back, shoulders and collar-bones, are pulling the head strongly backwards and downwards, thus over-riding the function of the sub-occipitals, and strapping the head firmly and immovably on to the body.

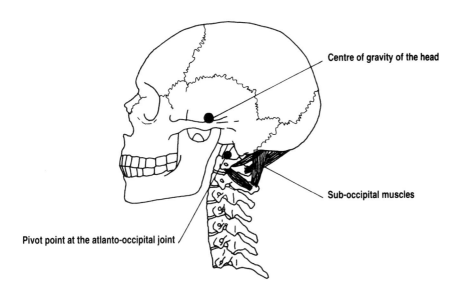

Centre of gravity of the head

Sub-occipital muscles

Pivot point at the atlanto-occipital joint

The subtle balancing act of the head on the neck is managed by the interaction of the extra weight in front of the pivot point and the small deep muscles which connect the skull with the neck (the sub-occipitals).

It is worth knowing how the brain achieves postural balance. The brain relies on information from the nervous system in achieving the ever-changing task of keeping the body upright. It relies heavily on receiving information from the nerve receptors in the neck muscles (which are particularly rich in nerve receptors, the deepest muscles having up to a hundred times more muscle spindles than most of our other muscles), together with information from our eyes and our balance organs in the inner ear.

When the sub-occipitals are not allowed to function properly, any subtle movement of the head becomes impossible. This lack of neck movement diminishes the nervous information fed to the brain, and contributes to the misuse of the body.

Pointing with the tips of your index fingers, try to locate the point where your head balances on your neck. Like most people you will probably aim too low and too far back. Move your finger-tips to the little groove just behind the ear lobes, and make tiny movements of your head and you may sense the articulation of the top joints. The point is really quite high up, level with the base of your nose.

LEFT: *Head poised and perfectly balanced on top of the spine.*

RIGHT: *Excessive tension in the neck muscles: a classic misuse.*

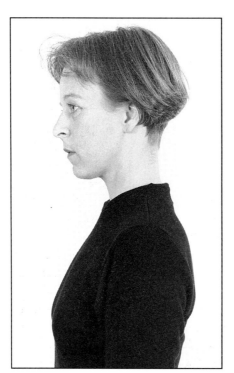

Good Use

When we talk about 'good use' in the physical sense, we are describing a condition where there is a good head/neck/back relationship, and balance and movement is achieved with a minimal amount of muscular tension. The muscular activity is distributed evenly throughout the body and there is an interaction and responsiveness between the muscle groups. This gives us an easy balance and fluidity of movement, freedom in our joints, full and unrestricted breathing and the best possible overall functioning in whatever activity we are engaged.

However, this condition comes about only as a result of 'good use' on a 'thinking' level. The term describes *the way* in which we use ourselves; good use is primarily being *conscious* of how our muscular system responds to our mental and emotional states and the demands made on us from the environment. It involves recognizing and being able to prevent any inappropriate and excessive muscular tensions occurring in response to these demands. The priority is to pay specific attention to maintaining a good relationship of the head, neck and back, thus ensuring an integrated and co-ordinated use of ourselves as a whole.

Misuse

Originally, when Alexander discovered that he was stiffening his neck and pulling his head back, and creating tension throughout his body, he thought that he was the only person to do this, but his investigations confirmed that this pattern of 'misuse' is common to the vast majority of people.

The effect of this misuse is that it interferes with the head/neck/back relationship, which means that a high degree of muscular tension is needed to maintain upright posture and for movement. This muscular tension is distributed unevenly through the body, with an excessive amount in some areas and too little tension in others, and there is a lack of interaction between the muscle groups. Obviously this brings about the very opposite of what we find with good use: being upright becomes an effort, there is a limited range of movement, the joints are stiff and breathing is impaired.

As with good use, misuse refers to our 'thinking'. It involves performing activities in a habitual and automatic way that is harmful to overall use and functioning. This could mean that we allow our emotional state to affect our musculature adversely, for example if we are worried about something we let tension build up in the neck muscles. Or it could be how we perform everyday activities. Observing people in action, we often see a great deal of effort being used, in parts of the body that are not directly

Good use: an even distribution of muscle tension, the various parts organized into a balanced whole.

Collapsed posture with head pulled back, chest collapsed, excessively curved lower back and knees locked.

Overtense posture with head strapped down on to neck, chest raised, extremely tight lower back and knees locked.

involved in the activity. Check for yourself how tightly you hold your toothbrush while cleaning your teeth – or how tightly you are holding this book right now! You will probably find that, like most people, you are using an excessive amount of effort in holding what is a very light object, and in a task that actually requires a minimum of force.

People misuse themselves in different ways. Broadly speaking, a person may hold himself up with too much tension – the 'sergeant major' approach – or he may 'collapse', with over-relaxed muscles. In practice, of course, it is not as clear cut as this; both forms of misuse involve a combination of excess tension and over-laxity. For example, even in someone with collapsed posture, only some muscles are 'over-relaxed', and therefore others have to work all the harder in compensation, and are over-tense.

An important proviso

The description of 'good use' above may give the impression that the aim in the Alexander Technique is to have a perfectly 'upright' spine. In fact, what we are looking for is an *improvement* of an individual's general condition. Using ourselves well actually refers to the quality of our thinking processes – and as such can be achieved by anyone in whatever physical condition. People may have structural conditions that for the most part cannot change; they may have a genetic condition that affects their musculo-skeletal system, such as scoliosis, an injury, or maybe years of built-up chronic tension. Improved use can still bring the rewards of increased freedom and ease in the movement patterns that are available.

The aim of the Alexander Technique is not, in fact, to achieve 'perfect posture'. 'Posture' is a word that Alexander teachers usually choose not to use, as this is most likely to make people pull themselves up into a 'sergeant major'-type posture – and this requires a lot of muscular effort. We use the term 'upright posture' to refer to one of our most striking features as human beings – our ability to stand upright and walk on two feet.

The word comfort comes from the latin com fortis *—* com *meaning 'with' and* fortis *meaning 'strong'. Sitting poised with the proper use of the primary control is comfortable — it gives us strength and yet there is no effort involved.*

Sitting in a collapsed fashion — usually associated with comfort — leads to fatigue, wear and tear. Slumping increases the pressure on the intervertebral discs of the spine by as much as three times compared to when the person is sitting in a balanced way.

Good Use Is Innate

How we use ourselves is to a large extent a matter of how we respond to the effect of gravity on our bodies. We have a complex and sophisticated system of postural reflexes and mechanisms which enable us to maintain our 'uprightness' – you could say they are part of our hardware – and this means that we have a natural potential for good use. When the primary control is working well, this inbuilt 'up direction' is facilitated to its maximum extent; in Alexander jargon we call this 'going up'. Unfortunately, when we misuse ourselves, pulling the head back and shortening the spine, we interfere with these mechanisms and stop them working so well. In Alexander jargon, we call this 'pulling down'.

Habitual Use

The way we use ourselves is largely a matter of habit, part of the programming that began the moment we were born, or perhaps even in the womb.

In order to acquire the necessary skills of life we learn by repeating an action many times until it becomes a habit, and we are then able to perform the action without having to think about it. With over six hundred muscles in our bodies and an infinite number of options and combinations of how to utilize them, our lives would come to a standstill if we had consciously to consider every movement we make. The great advantage here is that habit enables us to perform tasks more or less automatically while at the same time being able to give conscious thought and attention to other things.

The way we learn to drive is a good example. We all know how impossible driving seems to the beginner, with so many operations to perform at the same time. Yet with practice these functions become sufficiently automatic for us to be able to keep a watch on the traffic with ease. But, as every driver knows, we can learn bad habits of driving such as slamming in the gears or taking the corners too sharply. Just as with driving, we can also learn bad habits in our use, learning how to 'operate' ourselves inefficiently and potentially harmfully to our health and the proper functioning of ourselves.

The way in which we develop these habits is dependent on a variety of factors. As children we learn through imitation, copying people around us. Unfortunately if our peers, parents, and other role models have poor use, as well as imitating 'good' habits we will imitate the 'bad' habits. And as most

'Change involves carrying out an activity against the habit of life.'
F.M. Alexander

people are not set good examples by parents, poor use can begin at a very early age. In addition, we incorporate not only the physical movements but also the psychological attitudes of people around us. The intricate relationship of mind and body means that responses to mental concentration, emotional stress, anxiety and anger also become part and parcel of our habitual movement patterns.

Bad habits of movement and co-ordination can also develop because of physical disabilities or as a result of injury or illness. For example, the stress of coping with pain or the fear of tearing open a wound after an operation can make us produce tension which pulls the body out of shape and restricts normal movement. When someone has injured a leg or ankle they compensate by limping. Although strange at first, it soon becomes a habit which, because it has become the norm for them, they carry with them long after the injury has healed.

Very often someone's posture reflects an attitude they had about themself which is no longer appropriate. The woman who shot up in height quickly as a girl may now be of average height but she may still slouch because of that habitual misuse when she felt she was towering above her friends. These habits, accumulated over years, eventually become fixed patterns of tension in our bodies, which are reflected in our posture and the way we do things.

To give yourself a practical experience of how powerful the force of habit can be, as you sit here reading try folding your arms across your chest, in your usual way. Take a moment to 'feel' it and then look to see which arm is on top. Now unfold your arms and cross them again, this time with the other arm uppermost. What does that feel like? Was it easy to do? You probably found that, first, it was quite difficult to recross your arms the other way, and, second, it feels unfamiliar or even uncomfortable. Not only are we not aware of how automatically we do things like crossing arms, but we *seem* to have no choice but to do it our habitual way.

Unreliable Sensory Awareness

When Alexander tried to find a better way of using himself, he came upon a stumbling block. When he attempted to put his head in a different relationship to his spine, and then checked in the mirror he saw, to his dismay, that he was doing the complete opposite of what he 'felt' he was doing. Because of this he realized that he could not trust his sensory awareness of himself as a means of changing his use. It would be like using a tuning fork that was out of pitch to tune a piano – the whole piano would be out of tune. He called this phenomenon 'unreliable or faulty sensory awareness'.

It is well known that we have five senses through which we receive information about the outside world. Less well known is the fact that we have a sixth sense which gives us information about what is going on inside our bodies. This sensory awareness is properly called the 'kinaesthetic' sense or proprioception. Through this sense we should receive precise and accurate information about our position in space, where the various parts of us are in relation to each other, what the muscles are doing (the degree of tension and stretch in a muscle) and also movement. It is sometimes also referred to as our 'movement sense'. We receive this sensory input from nerve receptors in joints, ligaments, tendons and muscles.

If a person has poor use this kinaesthetic sense becomes dulled or inaccurate, for chronic tension in a muscle blocks and distorts the flow of correct information to the brain, and they are no longer able to feel that they are tense. In time a tense muscle or an incorrect position of a joint may even register as 'normal'. When things have gone this far, the correct use of muscles and joints may feel incorrect, unfamiliar, or even 'wrong'. For example, when someone has developed a habit of holding the head slightly tipped to one side, this will feel right to them. When this misuse is corrected, so that the head is carried more centrally, the person will feel that this is wrong.

In most of us our kinaesthetic sense is poorly developed, perhaps because we are mainly educated to use our visual and auditory senses (and taste). As already seen, when we neglect this sense it eventually becomes unreliable and can no longer be trusted to give us accurate sensory information about our bodies. We pay a high price for undervaluing this sense. We are no longer 'in touch' with our bodies, and therefore do not notice the early warning signals that we are misusing ourselves. We see the result of this in the extremely high incidence of use-related problems such as backaches and repetitive stress injuries in our society.

Try this to test the reliability of your sensory awareness. Stand in your normal way. Keeping your feet still, take a look at their position. They will most probably be slightly turned out. Close your eyes and attempt to put your feet in a position with the outside of the feet parallel. Register what it feels like and then open your eyes and take a look. What did it feel like? Are the feet in the position you felt them to be? Very few people actually manage to put their feet parallel and feel that they have. Usually the feet feel almost as if they are pointing inwards but in fact they are probably pointing outwards only a little less than before.

Stimulus–response

When Alexander was developing his technique, the stimulus–response theory of the Behaviourist school of psychology was in vogue. This posited that all behaviour came about as a response to a stimulus. Alexander was probably influenced by this way of looking at behaviour, and he came to understand that his unhelpful habits of muscular tension came about, not at random but in response to a definite stimulus. Moreover, this stimulus could be both external (for example, a loud noise) or internal – even the thought of reciting was enough of a stimulus to cause his neck and throat muscles to become tense.

This important discovery gave him a clue as to how he could change his habitual set responses, and in fact the Alexander Technique is primarily concerned with what happens between receiving a stimulus to act and the final response to the stimulus. We are constantly bombarded with both external and internal stimuli. As a consequence most of us spend a lot of our time in a state of over-excitation and our nervous systems become imbalanced. Alexander's great discovery is that we can indeed do something to redress this imbalance.

Constructive Conscious Control

From his lengthy observations of himself, Alexander ended up with what were several pertinent facts. His habits of use were unconscious and very deeply rooted, and he could not change them using what 'felt' right to him because his sensory awareness was untrustworthy. He also knew that his habitual misuse happened in response to a stimulus to do something.

Armed with these facts, he realized that instead of being ruled by habitual reactions he had to take back control of his actions and reactions on to a conscious plane. The word 'control' to many people implies some kind of restraint, but control in this sense is the freedom not to interfere with our natural reflex mechanisms for balance and movement, or in Alexander jargon 'to leave yourself alone'. This is a crucial point and one that is often misunderstood – it is through freedom that we gain control of our actions.

For Alexander, control is more akin to 'guiding' our use. The 'conscious guidance' he devised, which enabled him to replace his old unconscious habits of using himself with a new conscious way, were the thought processes of 'inhibition' and 'direction', to which we will now turn.

'How can the right thing happen if we are still doing the wrong thing? Obviously we have to stop doing the wrong thing first.'   *F.M. Alexander*

'Give yourself time to change the habits of a lifetime.'   *Claire*

Inhibition

The way Alexander used the word 'inhibition' is very different from the way Sigmund Freud, father of psychoanalytic theory, used it to describe an unhealthy suppression of emotions and memories. Alexander used inhibition in the physiological sense of the word, meaning the ability to 'switch off' a nervous impulse to a muscle.

Alexander realized that, in order to find a new way of using his voice, and himself as a whole, he first had to *stop* behaving in his habitual unconscious way. Real change could not happen by just overlaying a new pattern of behaviour on top of the old – this would be a form of suppression. He discovered *inhibition* – that he had to *stop* his habitual response to the stimulus to speak *before* it started. Inhibition is the skill that Alexander devised to give us the ability to prevent our unconscious habitual misuse.

When we go to do something, the muscles get ready in the way that they have learned to do that activity, in what you could call their habitual fashion. For instance, while you are waiting for a traffic light to turn green, you may notice that your muscles are 'getting ready' for you to drive off. Most of the time we do not notice this preparatory muscular activity because usually when we react to a stimulus we act very quickly and automatically. Inhibiting means that when we receive a stimulus to act, we pause momentarily to stop the habitual preparatory tension: this creates a space in which we have a choice about how we respond – we can go right ahead and

---

The next time the phone rings, take note of your habitual response. It is quite likely that you jump up immediately to answer it, and tighten your neck muscles and interfere with the 'primary control'. To change this way of reacting, you may instead like to think of a gentle voice saying, 'Hold on a minute,' and then give yourself time to choose how you use yourself to answer the phone. This may sound, though, as if were we to inhibit all the time we would never get anything done, but in practice it takes only a split second and actually gives us more time and energy as we stop rushing ahead of ourselves.

act habitually, do it differently or maybe choose to do nothing at all. It doesnot involve muscular effort, but is the mental decision not to react in our habitual way. By constantly practising inhibition in our everyday lives, we can gradually break the cycle of responding to a stimulus in a habitual way. The discovery that it is possible consciously to inhibit our initial reaction to a stimulus is what makes the Alexander Technique different from any other method of re-education. To Alexander inhibiting was not a negative but a positive process and the very cornerstone of his Technique.

Direction

'When I employ the words "direction" and "directed" with "use" in such phrases as "direction of my use" and "I directed my use", etc., I wish to indicate the process involved in projecting messages from the brain to the mechanisms and in conducting the energy necessary to the use of these mechanisms.' *F.M. Alexander*

Alexander realized that it was not enough to stop his habitual reaction to the stimulus to do something. He also had to encourage a better and different manner of using himself, when he eventually came to carry out the action. Having discovered that there were basic misuses of the body that were interfering with the primary control, he devised a set of 'directions' or mental 'orders' which are sent to counteract these misuses. They provide a new set of instructions to the body, the purpose of which is to bring about a better relationship of the head, neck and back and good use in all our actions. You could call this 'thinking into our bodies'.

Most of the time we are doing this unconsciously; that we are able to do anything at all, like standing up or moving, is because we are subconsciously giving ourselves a set of instructions (similar to a computer program) on how to do the activity. If our habitual use of ourselves is poor, it is because we are giving a set of instructions that is inappropriate or faulty (or maybe out of date) for performing an activity well.

Alexander's 'directions' are in the form of words that are, in fact, symbols of what happens on a muscular level. They usually read *Let the neck be free, so that the head can go forwards and up, so that the back can lengthen and widen, and let the knees go forwards and away*. It is important that they are given in this sequence, because each one occurs as a consequence of the preceding direction, and the release of one facilitates the release of the next. As Alexander says, we should give them 'all together, one after the other'.

Let the neck be free

This direction aims to send a fairly strong wish to the neck to release any unnecessary tension in the muscles, particularly those at the back which pull the head back and down into the shoulders (into a hunched position). It also addresses tension in the front of the neck, throat and jaw areas. This allows the head to be balanced and yet freely movable on top of the spine, rather than being forcibly gripped or strapped on to the spine.

So that the head can go forward and up

When we allow the neck to be free, the head, instead of being pulled 'backwards and downwards', is able to do the very opposite, i.e. go 'forwards and up'. This is not a direction in space, but a description of where the head is in relation to the neck. With a free neck, the head (which as we have seen is heavier in front of the pivot point, see diagram on page 15) is able to exert a gentle upwards pull on the neck muscles, and encourages a lengthening of the muscles along the rest of the spine.

When the head is going forwards and upwards a vital degree of movement at the first two joints of the spine is regained. The head is then free to make subtle adjustments to our balance, respond to stimuli it receives through its sense organs (for example you see something and turn your head to look at it), and is free to initiate the movement of the rest of the body.

So that the back can lengthen and widen . . .

With the release of the head forward and up, the back muscles are able to release. Pressure is taken off the intervertebral discs and there is a lessening of any excessive curvature of the spine. Consequently the whole of the spine lengthens, and this has a releasing effect on all of the muscles of the torso, causing a 'widening' or increase in the circumference of the torso. The ribcage is able to expand more freely, the lower back fills out, and the shoulders release and broaden.

Let the knees go forwards and away

This means to release the large strong muscles on the inside and back of the thighs which pull the knees in towards each other. The knees are allowed to go forwards from the lower back and away from each other, so that the knees are in line with the toes. When this happens there is also a release of the deep pelvic muscles and lower back. The legs can then work in co-ordination with the back, and assume a freer and more balanced attitude for both standing and moving.

'You cannot lengthen a person really, but you can in the sense of undoing the shortening.' *F.M. Alexander*

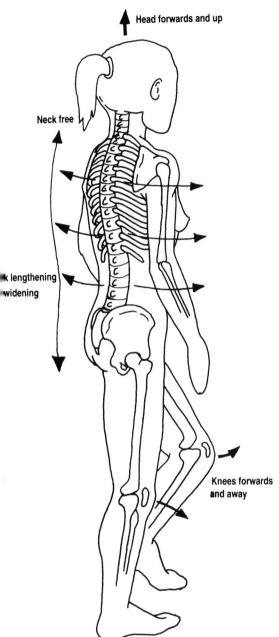

Head forwards and up

Neck free

lengthening
widening

Knees forwards
and away

DIRECTIONS
*These directions can be practised at any time
and in any situation; they are not dependent on
first getting into a specific position or posture.*

The Process of Directing

If you try the following exercise, you will experience how 'thinking into your body' affects muscle tone. As you are sitting reading this, rest one hand on your thigh. Now focus your attention on the index finger and imagine that you are pointing the finger at something, without actually moving the finger. You will notice that this finger now feels different from the other fingers. It may feel lighter or longer, and definitely will feel more alive. The difference you are feeling is a change in muscle tone.

The exercise above also gives you some experience of an aspect of directing that we call 'non-doing'. What we hope you will have noticed was that all you needed to do was 'think' about your finger and there was a change in muscle tone. It was quite different from actually lifting the finger to point. You did not have to move any muscles. You were simply sending a message from your brain to the muscle fibres.

The nature of the directions is 'non-doing', that is, not engaging with 'doing' thoughts which further tense our over-tense muscles. They must be thoughts or wishes, powerful and persuasive. Often when people are new to the Alexander Technique they think that they are giving directions, but in fact they are 'doing' them. For example, if their aim is to stand with better use, they try to *make* it happen by pulling themselves up with a great deal of unnecessary muscular effort. Instead, we achieve better standing by 'non-doing', that is, by simply giving our directions.

The aim is to think our directions creatively into the body, to establish new pathways for the necessary nervous impulse to the muscles. What takes place is a redistribution of muscle activity and a change in overall muscle tone.

'When you stop doing the wrong thing the right thing does itself.' *F. M. Alexander*

Inhibition and Direction in Practice

Although we present them as two separate skills, inhibition and direction could be described as a double-sided skill, like two sides of a coin. Inhibition stops at source the habitual reaction and creates the space for the directions. These thought processes have to be projected before an action, and continue through an action. (The phrase 'thinking in activity' was coined by philosopher and Alexander enthusiast John Dewey to refer to this.) If they are not, the old habitual way of doing something will reassert itself. Anyone who has taken lessons to improve a skill, for example tennis, will have noticed that when you are learning to do an activity in a new way, it is not enough to decide beforehand that you are going to do it differently. You have to pay attention continuously, otherwise you easily fall into your old patterns.

People often say that they cannot see how they will be able to inhibit and direct while they are doing something. As with learning any new skill, to begin with inhibiting and directing requires a lot of attention, and you have to take it slowly. But these are skills that you refine, and in time you will be able to do them very quickly and with only a small amount of attention, so that you are able to maintain conscious guidance of your use at the same time as performing the most complex of activities.

Improved Sensory Awareness

'Surely if it is possible for feeling to become untrustworthy as a means of direction, it should also be possible to make it trustworthy again.' *F. M. Alexander*

Alexander showed that it is possible to re-educate our sensory awareness so that it gives us full and accurate information. Like all of our six senses, the kinaesthetic sense works through a network of nerves. This network works well only when the muscles have a healthy tone and there is freedom in the joints, a condition that comes about when we have good use of ourselves. Once our use has improved, our kinaesthetic sense becomes more accurate and more reliable as a way of monitoring our use. With a trustworthy sensory awareness we can, at a very early stage, be aware of any tension that is harmful to our overall use, and can then choose to release that unwanted tension. This creates a 'virtuous' as opposed to a 'vicious' circle. Improved use leads to a better sensory awareness, which in turn leads to an improved use of ourselves, and so forth.

In practice, therefore, what we learn in the Alexander Technique is to give a small part of our attention to our kinaesthetic sense, in an ongoing way, during all our activities. If we notice that we are misusing ourselves we pay more attention to our use, and correct it by inhibiting any misuses and giving directions. We do this most of the time, with all our other senses anyway. We may have the radio on as background music, not paying much attention to it, and yet if one of our favourite songs is played we notice and can give it more attention. A mother is particularly adept at this. If she is busy with some intricate task in one room, with her children in another where she cannot keep an eye on them, she will keep her attention on them. If suddenly they become suspiciously quiet, or one of them is upset, she will instantly be aware of it.

Our kinaesthetic sense awakened, we become more acutely aware and feel more alive. One student talked about how pleasurable it was to experience herself walk, what fun it was to feel the movement in her legs, so much so that she would offer to go out and get the evening paper, just to enjoy her body in movement.

Sense of self

Our kinaesthetic sense is not only the basis of balance, posture and movement, it is also the basis in a very real way of our sense of self. Although our 'self' encompasses our minds, feelings and perhaps some sense of a spiritual identity, we do not exist without our bodies.

Because of this, the way we use ourselves is very closely bound up with who we are, or who we think we are. We say things like 'I *am* round-shouldered', when it would perhaps be more accurate to say 'I am rounding my shoulders'; basically, we identify on a deep level with being round-shouldered, and therefore changing our use can mean having to change our self-perception too.

Many people find that as their kinaesthetic sense increases, they have a stronger sense of their own identity. A common response during lessons is 'I feel like I've come home'. What they are experiencing is coming home into their own bodies.

Choice

For many people the idea of having choice in their lives is a purely philosophical notion. In Alexander Technique we learn to undo chronically held muscular tensions, and come to realize that we can change what we thought were 'natural' and unchangeable habits of movement and posture over which we had no control. When people have this very practical

'Change involves carrying out an activity against the habit of life.'
F. M. Alexander

'Thus it will be seen that the difference between the new habit and the old is that the old was our master and ruled us, whilst the new is our servant ready to carry out our lightest wish without question, though always working quietly and unobtrusively on our behalf.' *F. M. Alexander*

experience of having choice and individual responsibility in how they use their bodies, very often their whole outlook on life changes as they realize it applies to all facets of their being. They are able to respond to life not as creatures of habit but, through consciousness, to open up the possibility for more appropriate, less stressful and ultimately more creative choices.

End-gaining and Means Whereby

Two more concepts that are fundamental to the Alexander Technique are 'end-gaining' and 'means whereby'. By end-gaining Alexander meant that we are so exclusively focused on reaching our desired goal that we do not consider how we get there; more specifically, we do not pay attention to our use. We automatically adopt our habitual misuse, and carry out the activity with unnecessary effort and tension. This principle of end-gaining is what keeps us locked into unconscious and automatic behaviour, according to Alexander.

He suggested that instead we should follow the 'means whereby' approach, that is, the reasoned means to the gaining of an end. Our primary focus should be on the process by which we reach our goal, not on the goal itself. In so doing we will give ourselves time to become aware of our habitual response, and be able to work out the steps by which we can best reach our goal. In practice this involves inhibiting the habitual way of acting, and consciously projecting new directions, paying attention to our use throughout each of the steps involved in reaching the goal. In this way the old habits of misuse can be broken and new and improved use can be established.

Having Alexander Lessons

Having an intellectual understanding of Alexander's work is not generally thought to be enough to enable you to practise Alexander's ideas. Of course, it is possible to teach yourself about the primary control, as Alexander did, but it took him many years to achieve what an Alexander teacher could show you in a matter of minutes. Therefore we recommend that you attend lessons in order to gain the experience that will make the concepts come alive for you.

Lessons are normally taught on a one-to-one basis and last 30–45 minutes. They consist of lying-down work, standing and sitting, breathing, walking and other activities. The teacher's role is to help the student increase her awareness of, and to co-ordinate, her thinking and her movements, by guiding her through the movements and activities towards an understanding of exactly how mental and muscular habits make up so much of our postural patterns. Using her hands in a light and non-intrusive way, and verbal instructions where appropriate, the teacher will make a few minor alterations to the balance of the head, neck and back of the student, bringing about a release of tension. The student will be instructed to do nothing in response to the idea of making a movement, and the teacher will then initiate the movement, before the student has a chance to let her habitual reaction come into play. The student will thus learn to break with habitual ways of using herself and gain an experience of a new and improved use.

Students often report a sense of lightness and ease, and that it felt as if neither they not the teacher actually 'did' anything. Indeed, the role of the student *is* to do nothing, and instead be open to a new experience. Handing over responsibility to the teacher to facilitate good use does not mean, however, that you no longer need to attend to what is going on. On the contrary, you will be encouraged to remain alert, keep your eyes open, and to 'listen' to what is going on in your body. This way learning becomes

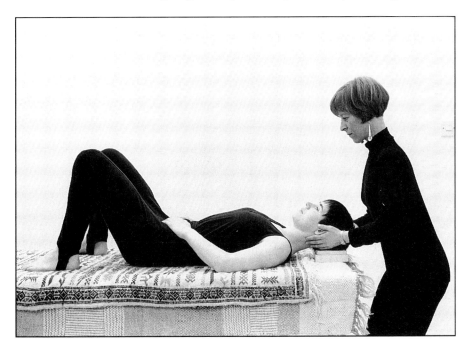

Lessons are usually experienced as being gentle and relaxing but are also mentally challenging and stimulating.

a co-operative process between the student and the teacher. Gradually, you learn to monitor your own use and to use the skills of inhibition and direction, as the teacher hands over more of the responsibility to you. Although you have a teacher to help you, you must ultimately make your own discoveries and make the Technique your own.

After some months of lessons your body may begin to change shape, your clothes may no longer fit you in the same way as before, and you may have 'grown' taller. The benefits people discover are not only physical: students find that their thinking and their emotional responses change too, and they often gain confidence.

People can continue with lessons for several years, in part because of the beneficial nature, in part because they are enjoyable and relaxing. Some people need only a handful of sessions before grasping what they need to know. The traditional thinking is that most people need between twenty and thirty to benefit from the Technique, but individuals, and the approach of the individual teacher, vary.

'The Alexander lessons made me aware of my body, of my breathing and of my posture for the first time in my life. I became more aware of my body as part of myself and thus grew more aware of Chia growing inside me. When friends asked me what the Technique was all about, I was hard pressed to explain it – to explain how it made me feel better with and in myself. When I talked about letting the neck be free and using my back to breathe, they looked at me as if I was mad. I don't think until you've had "hands-on" you can appreciate just how "freeing" it can be.' *Francine*

2 | The Alexander Technique in Practice

Alexander Procedures for Pregnancy and Labour

'The aim of re-education on a general basis is to bring about at all times and for all purposes, not a series of correct positions or postures, but a co-ordinated use of the mechanisms in general.' *F.M. Alexander*

In this chapter we introduce the basic Alexander Technique procedures that we teach to all Alexander students whether they are pregnant or not. These comprise the 'monkey', squatting, lunging, kneeling, and all fours. We show you how these procedures can be used in pregnancy and during labour, the benefits of practising them, and include both active and resting positions.

These procedures encourage you to use your body so that the head/neck/back relationship is operating most effectively; this facilitates good use and enables the body to function well. Because they are being presented in a book, it may appear that we are teaching a series of static positions, but it is important to appreciate that these are procedures that show you how to use your body well in *movement*.

During your pregnancy we recommend that if you are having lessons you ask your teacher to take you through these procedures so that you can integrate them as much as possible into your daily life. Using them will help you maintain your good use and you will also find that everyday activities, which become quite difficult because of carrying the extra weight of the baby, are in fact much easier if you use your body in this way. These procedures are also extremely effective for alleviating discomforts caused by the weight and position of the baby, such as muscular aches, heartburn and breathlessness.

In Western culture, our muscles and joints are not accustomed to most of these movements. For example, most women nowadays are unable to squat because our modern lifestyles simply do not give us either the need or the opportunity for squatting as part of our daily routine. These procedures will also encourage the release of muscles and joints which make the process of childbirth easier. If you want to use them in labour, you will need to practise beforehand. By the time you go into labour we like you to have a repertoire of positions that you can practise with ease. If your partner also practises these positions he can help you during pregnancy and labour by suggesting alternatives if you cannot think what would be best for you.

A facet of Western culture is the belief that childbirth is dangerous and painful. The fear and tension that this attitude engenders is what most hinders the birth process. Practising these procedures, women develop a trust and confidence in their bodies' ability to give birth. They discover an instinctive sense of themselves that is vital in labour, allowing the involuntary process of birth to occur. Of course some women have this instinctive approach to birth without prior preparation but, sadly, for many it is something they need consciously to learn. Even if the birth does not turn out the way you had hoped, and the procedures cannot be used, you will still have learned a better use of your body. These skills are also invaluable for the demanding role of caring for your newborn baby, and they will remain with you for the rest of your life.

In Chapter 7 you will find variations of these movements and positions that we recommend you use during labour and birth.

The Monkey

'There is no such thing as a right position, but there is such a thing as a right direction.' *F.M.Alexander*

In Alexander Technique we learn a procedure that has come to be called the 'monkey' in Alexander jargon; if you look at the photograph on page 36 you can easily see why. It is actually a semi-squat, the depth of which can be anywhere between standing upright and going down to a full squat.

The 'monkey' is a very efficient way of using your body. Because the head and knees going forwards counterbalances the bottom going backwards over the heels (creating what Alexander called 'antagonistic muscular action'), a minimum amount of muscular effort is required. This uses less energy and is therefore less tiring, and it also gives a greater degree of flexibility, mobility and elasticity through the body.

In monkey the head/neck/back relationship is working at its best, allowing the body to work in a co-ordinated way, with proper use of all parts of the body. The muscles at the front and back of the torso are allowed to lengthen, giving more freedom of movement in the ribcage and diaphragm, which allows full and proper breathing. In monkey the legs have less tension throughout, and consequently there is more freedom in the joints, as these weight-bearing joints – ankles, knees and hips – are near the midpoint of their movement range. At the top of the back the arms hang freely from the shoulder girdle, functioning as extensions of the muscles in the back.

All the other Alexander procedures are based on the same body mechanics as the monkey and give the same advantages as regards the functioning of the body. A squat is a very deep monkey; a lunge is a monkey with one leg in front of the other; kneeling is a monkey in which your knees and calves form the base for the monkey; all fours is a monkey in which you are supported by all four limbs.

Using 'monkey' in everyday life

The monkey is not a static position; rather, it is a way to use the body that requires the least muscular effort, and in which you have the most flexibility and mobility. Ideally if we used ourselves correctly we would automatically go into some form of monkey for almost all activities in our lives. When we go from sitting to standing or standing to sitting in a correct way we move through the monkey. It should be used for everyday activities such as bending, picking something up, lifting, standing at a work surface, brushing our teeth, etc.; it is also useful as a way to relieve a stiff back if you have been standing for a long time. Monkey has a place in martial arts, and various sports such as golf, tennis, skating, skiing, etc.

In monkey, using the back as a whole and with the primary control working well the conditions are optimum for the most skilful use of our hands, be it for drawing, painting, washing up, writing, playing an instrument, or doing any kind of precise and fine work – or handling a small baby.

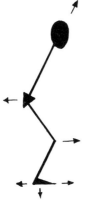

The head and knees going forwards in monkey counterbalance the bottom going backwards over the heels.

MONKEY INSTRUCTIONS

What you do in preparation for the monkey is vital. Before proceeding, give your directions to *let your neck be free, so that the head can go forward and up, in such a way that the back lengthens and widens and the knees are free to go forward and away.* During the whole of this procedure you should keep your eyes alert and not let them glaze over or fix vacantly on some point.

Stand with the feet slightly turned out, about shoulder width apart. The weight of the body should be distributed between the front and back of the feet. You may like to check that the weight is falling through

the heels as there is a common tendency to lean forwards over the toes.

Initiate the movement into monkey with a slight further release of the head forwards, and tilt forwards from the hip joints, keeping your head, neck and back in one piece. At the same time release your hips, knees and ankle joints to let the knees bend forwards. Allow the back to widen and the arms to hang freely from the shoulder girdle.

It is very important that you never think of bending down when doing a monkey, as this is all too likely to trigger habits of excessive muscular contraction. Unnecessary tightening of the muscles over the hips, knees and ankles will restrict the freedom of movement of these joints.

As you come back to the upright position, keep your weight over the heels, and continue to direct your head forwards and up. Take extra care not to pull your head back and lock the knees as you complete the movement.

Monkey with hands on table
This basic Alexander procedure (*right*) teaches how to use the arms as an extension of the back (see page 138), and how to keep the hands and arms free of unwanted tension. This is an extremely useful movement for labour.

Dividing the weight between the hands and the feet helps you to release tightening in the legs and pelvic floor. It is a good way to free the breathing mechanism. You can also try rocking gently backwards and forwards. Take care not to hunch your shoulders, and do not lean heavily on the table.

The Lunge

This movement is similar to monkey in that the back is slightly inclined forwards, the knees are bent and the feet are hip width apart, but here one foot is placed in front and one behind. The legs thus provide a strong base for shifting the upper body forwards or backwards.

The lunge should be used for any activity where you need to either push or pull something. Using a lunge, the strength for the movement comes from the legs and the back moving together

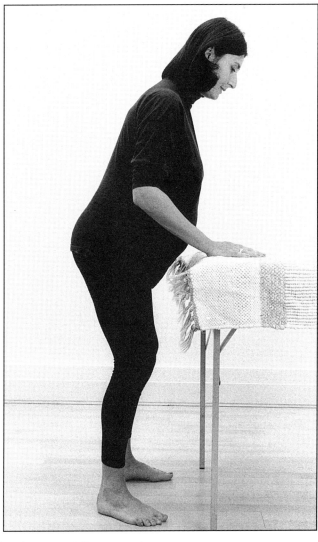

in one piece, with the arms and hands used only in a guiding capacity. Domestic tasks – such as ironing, vacuuming, opening doors or standing at a work surface preparing food – require this movement, as do sports such as tennis, fencing, t'ai chi and aikido. In many instances it is also a more stable position to use than a squat when lifting a heavy object from the floor. The lunge is also useful in labour. As it is an upright position it is more suitable for the earlier stages.

LUNGE INSTRUCTIONS

While practising this exercise, it is important to keep the sense of your head, neck and torso being in one integrated piece, allowing your arms to hang freely from the shoulder joints. The hips, knees and ankle joints must be free at all times.

Begin in a very shallow monkey. Allow your upper body to move to the right, so that your weight is now on your right foot, and the left foot feels 'empty'. Now put your left foot forwards and slightly to the left with the toe pointing straight ahead. Your back foot should be at about a 45-degree angle.

Now let your left knee move forwards over the toe, and at the same time allow the whole of your torso to glide forwards so that most of your weight is over the front foot and the back leg is now your 'empty' leg. Remember that your back leg should still be slightly bent.

Thinking strongly into your left heel, allow your upper body to shift back on to your back leg again. It will need to bend more, whilst the front knee will be in a shallower bend.

You can now play with shifting the weight of your upper body backwards and forwards from one leg to the other. The movement is often easier if you visualize your pelvis moving forwards and backwards.

Alternate your lunge practice between right leg forward and left leg forward.

Squatting

The benefits of having an active labour are now increasingly being recognized, and squatting is one of the activities most often recommended. In some cultures, people squat for many activities, especially sitting, and consequently can do so comfortably, maintaining the position for long stretches of time. In Western societies, probably because of the furniture used, people do not tend to squat as part of their everyday life. Because of this, the majority cannot squat correctly, even for a short period. It is therefore an unrealistic and unfair expectation that women should be able to squat to give birth, without prior preparation.

As toddlers we can squat easily, but we tend to lose this ability through lack of practice as we get older. To be able to squat, the hip, knee and ankle joints have to be very flexible. Regaining this flexibility involves releasing muscles and tendons that have been habitually over-contracted, probably since we were children. This is possible but it does take a lot of practice, which is one reason why Alexander lessons should be started as early as possible in pregnancy – if possible before. You should practise squatting a lot during pregnancy – on you own or with support.

In Alexander lessons, we start by teaching the student the monkey or semi-squat, and then gradually encourage them to deepen this until they are able to adopt a full squatting position while maintaining all their directions.

SQUATTING INSTRUCTIONS

Follow the instructions for monkey but with the feet wider apart. Inhibit – the very thought of bending to lower yourself is a strong stimulus to 'end-gain'. Give yourself time to stop and reconsider the means whereby you will get there.

While making sure that you keep your heels on the floor, that your back is lengthening and widening, and that your knees are going away from each other, bend at the hips, knees and ankles to allow yourself to lower into a deeper squat.

It is important that you only go into as deep a squat as you can manage while maintaining all these conditions. When you have gone as far as you can, do not give up your upward direction and slump into the squat, as that would make it difficult to come up again.

To get up from the squat, allow the head to release a little further forward while at the same time letting your back come back over the heels. This will create the necessary antagonistic stretch in the muscles to allow you to rise again without having to push with your legs. You will simply 'fall upwards'.

'Good' squatting
If you are squatting well, your neck is free, your back is lengthening and widening, your knees are going away from each other and your heels are firmly on the ground.

'Poor' squatting
You will not benefit from squatting if you are pulling your head back, rounding your back, or allowing your heels to come off the floor. You should also avoid pulling your knees in towards each other, as you will be tightening the thigh muscles and pelvic floor.

Sitting on a low stool or books
This is effectively a squat and encourages the release and stretch of your inner thighs and pelvic floor. In pregnancy it is a comfortable way to sit as the baby gets bigger, and a good resting position for labour. (A pile of telephone books gives a good broad base, the height of which is easily adjustable.)

Hanging squat

The safest way to practise squatting and help increase flexibility and suppleness in the joints of the legs is by using the handles of a half-open door (or a secure rail) for support. Do check that the door handles are well secured before you start. We call it the 'hanging squat'.

Stand, feet apart, a little less than arm's length away from the edge of the door (or rail), and take hold of the handles. Give your directions and release your weight backwards to let the arms come to a full stretch, but without rounding your shoulders. Release your knees forward as you lower your bottom towards the heels. You will now be, as it were, hanging from your arms, with more of your weight back over your heels than you would be able to do in an unsupported squat.

To return to the upright position, release a little further into the hanging squat and give your directions to lengthen and widen. Do not pull with your arms. Keeping these directions going, together with the intention to stand up again, should be all that is required.

Hanging squat holding on to door handles, bar or rail
In this squat much of the body weight is supported by your hands, making it easier to release tension in the legs. This is an excellent way of learning to squat.

Counterbalanced squatting

Follow the 'hanging squat' instructions for this, but instead of holding on to door handles you will be holding on to your partner.

You can either both go into full squat or your partner can use a shallow monkey or lunge position (see page 38). Maintaining eye contact and smiling will help you to stay alert and keep your breathing full and unrestricted. It is important here that you can trust your partner to take your weight as you lean away from each other. Building up this trust is useful practice for your partner's role during labour.

Counterbalanced squatting
This 'hanging squat' (*above*) is useful for learning to trust each other, as the weight of one person counterbalances the other. It is not particularly helpful for the actual labour.

Supported by partner in a lunge position
Squatting with your partner in a lunge (*right*) is a more stable version of the 'hanging squat'.

Kneeling

Kneeling is a useful alternative to squatting for many activities that take place on the ground. Kneeling positions are commonly used in an active and upright labour. You can either kneel in an upright position (*right*), or sit with your bottom on your heels. Practising these positions during pregnancy will also prepare you for the birth and for after the baby is born, for changing nappies on the floor or playing with the baby.

KNEELING INSTRUCTIONS

First, stand in your normal position. Let your weight shift back over the heels to help free up the hips, knees and ankles. Direct your neck to be free and your head forwards and up, as you incline your torso slightly forwards from the hips, and take a small step back with one foot. Go down on to one knee, and then incline your torso a little further forwards. Next send your hips back to enable you to go down on to the other knee. Your knees will need to be about hip width apart. Be careful not to adopt an over-tense 'sergeant-major' stance.

With bottom on heels sitting upright
This is a restful and supportive position that helps you to work on releasing the pelvic floor and muscles of the inner thighs. If your partner sits on a chair behind you, you can rest your arms on his knees.

All Fours

In four-legged animals it is easy to see the integrated working of the head, neck and back and how the limbs are co-ordinated around this 'central mechanism'.

During a course of Alexander lessons, your teacher may at some stage introduce you to the all fours position and crawling. These are helpful procedures in that they encourage the lengthening and widening of the back, and develop the co-ordination of the use of the limbs with the head, neck and back.

Basic all fours – 'good use'

To benefit fully from this position, your head, neck and back need to be in line, and your weight evenly distributed over all four limbs. The joints in the arms and legs should be free to move.

All fours – 'misuse'
Common misuses are pulling the head back or allowing the head and neck to drop, letting the lower back sag, and locking the joints in the legs and arms.

ALL FOURS INSTRUCTIONS

You can get into this position from lying down by rolling over on to your side, and then going on to all fours. Alternatively, you can start by kneeling, then move your bottom towards the heels, incline your head and torso forwards, and 'walk' your hands in front until you are on all fours.

Take a moment to be conscious of your back in this position. You should be looking straight down at the floor, the heels of your hands should be directly below your shoulder joints and your knees below your hip joints. Because of the size of your 'bump' the knees may need to be a little wider apart. To get up from all fours, move your bottom back towards your heels and raise yourself into a kneeling position and then stand up.

Rocking and circling on all fours

In pregnancy we teach women how to rock backwards and forwards and also use a circling movement while on all fours. This is very good for alleviating backache. It eases out excessive tension in the lumbar spine and strengthens the back. During labour women instinctively use rocking and circling movements because it eases the pain. Physiologically they help the rotation and descent of the baby in the pelvis.

Once on all fours, check that the head, neck and back are in alignment and that the back is neither arched nor hollowed. The wrists, elbows and shoulders, and ankles, knees and hips should be freely movable.

For rocking, pivot at the knees and the wrists, allowing the head and torso to move backwards and forwards over the limbs. For circling, again pivot at the knees and wrists, but allow the torso to move forwards with the crown of the head leading, then move to the side, then backwards, then to the other side, until you have described a full circle. During contractions this circling movement can be gentle or more vigorous if the pain is intense.

Dynamic Resting the Alexander Way

Being up and about for long periods puts a great strain on our backs. The combination of the force of gravity and the downward pull from excessive muscular tension jams our joints together and compresses the bones of the spine. It is no wonder that, at the end of the day, we are appreciably shorter than when we get up in the morning, and that as we get older we gradually lose our full height.

Fortunately there is an Alexander 'habit' that not only encourages a dynamic head/neck/back relationship and good use, but also revitalizes your spine. The habit is to lie in the semi-supine position, which you can see demonstrated in the photograph on page 50. This simple and effective habit should be as essential a part of your everyday life as brushing your teeth. It has the advantage of being something that you can do for yourself to improve your well-being, even if you do not have lessons. Lying down in semi-supine provides you with the opportunity to take time, to stop and 'un-do' excessive tension, and makes you more aware of your back – this position alone will release unnecessary tension in your muscles and joints.

One of the major advantages of this position is its beneficial effect on the spine. In between each two bones of the spine (except between the top two and in the sacrum and coccyx) there is a spongy elastic 'cushion' with a fluid-filled centre called an 'intervertebral disc'. These discs make up one-quarter of the spine; they act as shock absorbers for our everyday movements, and assist in giving the spine strength and flexibility. Pressure on these discs, from the effect of gravity while upright or from misalignment of the spine, causes these discs to be flattened and consequently the spine loses its shock-absorbing qualities and flexibility. If the spine is extremely misaligned or compressed, the disc protrudes and presses on the surrounding tissues, and in advanced cases puts pressure on a nerve route running from the spine. This is what is popularly called a 'slipped disc'. In the semi-supine position, the gentle stretch on the spine causes the bones to ease away from each other, and the discs can then plump up and regain their elasticity and optimum shape.

In semi-supine, the head is supported on a small pile of books which puts a gentle stretch on the muscles of the back of the neck, and encourages a release of the tension in these muscles and consequently throughout the length of the spine. Having the knees bent allows a release of the muscles lying deep in the pelvis, and in the lower back. This passive stretch reduces any excessive curves in the spine and allows the torso to spread out and widen on to the floor.

You need to lie down for about twenty minutes at least once a day. Twice a day is even better, so an ideal routine would be at lunchtime and then again in the evening. This gives your body a welcome rest every four to five hours. Although it may seem an excessive amount of time to take out of a busy day, it actually creates more time for you, because you will feel refreshed, alert and energized afterwards. You will find that a short time resting in this way makes you feel deeply relaxed and is far more beneficial than a catnap. If, on the other hand, you find that you are always wanting to fall asleep while resting in semi-supine, it is probably a sign that

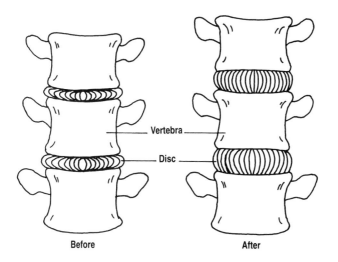

Vertebra

Disc

Before

After

Intervertebral discs before and after lying in semi-supine.

you would be better off getting some proper sleep. Some people also like to do a session last thing at night to ease out the tensions of the day so that they enjoy a more relaxed sleep.

Although semi-supine is often called a resting position, it could be more correctly described as 'dynamic resting'. You do not simply lie passively, allowing yourself to drift off. It is rather a combination of being physically still and 'quiet', allowing the books and floor to support your weight, and yet mentally being alert and active. It is a time when you can practise inhibiting any unnecessary tension and giving directions, and develop your skills of self-observation. Semi-supine is a time you put aside when you don't have to concentrate on your everyday activities and can devote your attention exclusively to practising these Alexander skills.

One word of warning. Towards the end of pregnancy it is not advisable to lie flat on the back. In this position, the weight of the uterus falls directly on to one of the major blood vessels that returns blood to the heart. This produces a fall in the blood pressure in the mother, and a reduced supply of oxygenated blood going to the baby. Dizziness, lightheadedness or shortness of breath are signs to look out for. See later in this chapter for some alternative resting positions to use.

Lying Down

You should lie on a firm surface, either on a rug or a carpeted floor, not on a bed or other soft surface as this will give inadequate support to the parts of the body designed to bear weight. We suggest that you wear comfortable, loose-fitting clothes.

You will need an inch or more in soft paperback books to rest your head upon. The height of books varies from person to person, depending on several factors including shape and length of the neck, shape of head and upper back, and on the amount of tension in the neck and upper back. If you are trying this on your own, use sufficient books to give a subtle stimulus to the neck muscles to lengthen; that is, your head should not be tilted back – it should be slightly rotated forwards. If you have too many books you may feel pressure on the front of the throat making you feel as if you want to swallow. If you are not sure how many books to use, it is better to err on the generous side. For the best guide, consult a trained Alexander teacher.

When deciding to lie down in semi-supine it pays to take a little time to consider how to go from the vertical to the horizontal plane. Your teacher will probably instruct you about this, but here we will describe one way that we find particularly useful.

LYING DOWN (OR SEMI-SUPINE) INSTRUCTIONS

Place your books on the floor. Stand approximately the length of your torso plus about 30cm away from the books and spend a few moments becoming aware of releasing tension in your neck and back and in your legs. Next, lower yourself to the ground. There are several ways you can approach this; perhaps the most regularly used method is by first coming down on to one knee and then the other, and then by bending at the hips, knees and ankles. Sit down on your heels and move your bottom to one side to place the legs in front.

You will now be sitting with your bottom in line with the books so that when you lie down your head will finish up resting on the books. Bend your knees placing your feet flat on the floor.

Place your hands palm down on the floor behind you and lean backwards, supporting your back with your hands. Now lower your back, in one piece, towards the floor, bending your arms so that you can rest first on one elbow, then on both. Take your time, and make sure that you are making use of the support of your arms rather than using your abdominal muscles, and that you are not holding your breath, stiffening your neck, hunching your shoulders or holding on for dear life with your legs.

(In pregnancy, especially as you get bigger, it might be easier to first lie on your side and then roll over on to your back. This is particularly advisable if you suffer from backache, as it puts less strain on the back.)

A way of preventing tightening the muscles in the neck is to move one hand to support your head, while resting on the other forearm, as you then lower your head on to the pile of books. Make sure that it is only the bony part at the back of your head (the occiput) that is in touch with the surface. The neck should not be touching the books as this would make it hard for the muscles to release.

Now check the position of the feet and legs. The legs should be able to balance in this position with minimum muscular effort, falling neither together nor apart. If your legs aren't in balance you may need to bring your heels closer towards your bottom, so that they are roughly a foot away from your buttocks and about shoulder width apart. In the beginning it may feel difficult to direct the knees up to the ceiling, but gradually, as your back releases and spreads out on to the floor, the unnecessary tightening in the legs will ease, and it will be much more comfortable.

Now place your hands on your abdomen with the elbows on the floor, pointing out away from the body. Let your hands lie open and

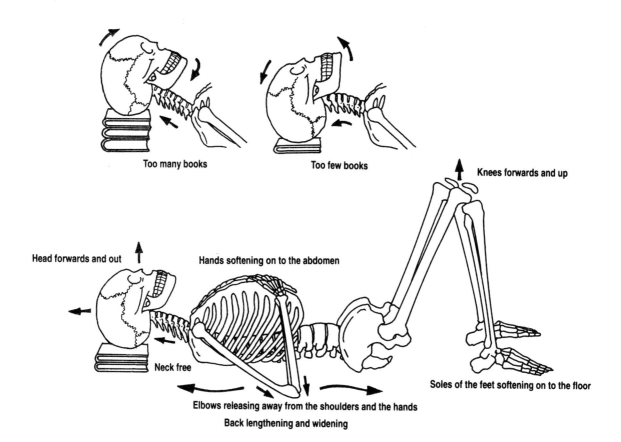

Too many books

Too few books

Knees forwards and up

Head forwards and out

Hands softening on to the abdomen

Neck free

Soles of the feet softening on to the floor

Elbows releasing away from the shoulders and the hands

Back lengthening and widening

Directions in semi-supine

not touching each other. Keep your eyes open and focused and alert to stop yourself from becoming drowsy, and think through your Alexander directions. If you find that you drift away and begin to mind-wander, 'inhibit', gently bringing your awareness back to your contact with floor and books, and go through your directions again.

The aim of being in semi-supine is not to flatten the lower back by pushing it down towards the floor but only to take the pressure off the spine, allowing it to release. We are all shaped differently, and some people may 'feel' the whole of the back when first attempting this, while others will take longer to sense a release down towards the floor.

Getting Up

When you get up from semi-supine you should take care how you move, so that you do not lose the muscular release you have acquired. If you were to rise by lifting your head first, you would tighten the neck muscles excessively; it is better to roll over on to your side. First choose which side you are going towards and look in that direction by moving your eyes only. Allow your head to turn in that direction, then let your body follow, at the same time bringing your arm across your body and placing your hand flat on the floor. From this position you can bring yourself up on to all fours, still keeping your awareness of your head, neck and back, working all in one piece. Once on all fours take a moment to become conscious of your head/neck/back relationship before moving your bottom back towards your heels and raising yourself into a kneeling position before standing.

PART TWO

The Alexander Way for Pregnancy

In this part of the book we will look at the changes that are continually taking place in a woman's body and lifestyle during pregnancy, and suggest ways in which the Alexander Technique can make it easier to accommodate these changes, and also help prevent the complaints that commonly occur in pregnancy.

Why Alexander is Important

Pregnancy is one of the most stressful experiences, both physically and emotionally, that a woman will live through. The physical problems posed by the growing baby, which profoundly alters the way most women move for several months, create the potential for many aches and pains, as well as more severe ailments such as heartburn and varicose veins. If your use is poor, then pregnancy will undoubtedly exacerbate all your postural imbalances, thus increasing the likelihood of problems. The Alexander Technique will help you to come to terms with how your body is changing, and to develop 'useful' postural habits to enable you to move as freely as possible. The improved use will also make it less likely that you will suffer the common complaints of pregnancy.

You will also be able to reduce your own stress levels by learning to monitor your muscular tensions and to unwind. This has a quietening effect on the nervous system, and has a beneficial effect on all the systems in the body: breathing becomes freer, blood pressure is reduced, and circulation and digestion are improved. Your stress threshold, i.e. your capacity to cope with stress, will gradually rise. This is invaluable preparation for the labour.

Pregnancy is often an emotionally challenging period. Alexander work can help you to understand the connection between your emotions and your body, which will help you maintain an inner balance and centredness. You will also benefit from the fact that *your* needs, as well as the baby's, are being looked after, as it is a common experience in pregnancy for all the focus of attention to fall on to the baby and for the mother to be ignored.

One of the positive side effects of pregnancy is that women develop an increased body awareness. This is partly due to necessity – the pure mechanics of carrying around up to an extra 9–13 kilograms forces you into thinking about how you are doing things – and partly due to the increased sensitivity that you gain from having a new life growing inside you. You could say that you have opened up a new channel of communication between the mind and body, which makes it easier to learn to 'listen' to your body, and to give directions. This new body awareness, coupled with the effects of progesterone (see page 57), means that, on the whole, pregnant women learn the Technique easily, and habitually fixed patterns of misuse can change relatively quickly.

When to Have Lessons

Ideally, we recommend that you have Alexander lessons before becoming pregnant, as your new good use will then already be in operation before the changes associated with pregnancy begin. However, in reality pregnancies are often not so well planned, teachers might not be available locally, or you might never have heard of the work until well into your pregnancy.

If this is the case, the earlier in your pregnancy you start having lessons the better. (Lessons are not strenuous; the Technique does not put one at risk of miscarriage, at any stage in pregnancy.) Learning the Alexander Technique is a gradual process and it does take time for one's use to be affected positively. It is also preventive, so the earlier you can start, the more likely you are to avoid suffering many of the discomforts of pregnancy. Having said this, there are still many benefits to be gained even if you begin lessons later on in pregnancy.

When you look for a teacher, it is worth trying to find someone who has experience of working with pregnant women, because they will know about the specific demands that childbearing makes on you, and the particular benefits that the Technique can offer. However, don't worry if you cannot find one in your area; all Alexander teachers work with the same principles, and you can complement the work in your lessons with information in this book on the specific application of the Technique to pregnancy and childbirth.

What you learn in lessons will also help after the birth, and in fact it is probably then that you will appreciate it the most, when you are facing so many new situations and demands. Learning the Technique for pregnancy and childbirth is not an end in itself. What you learn is for life and for every activity in life.

'This is the most important thing I've done for myself in a long time. If any woman is going to be a multiparous mother [have four or more children in a short space of time] she must learn the Alexander Technique to regain and re-adapt her body and herself between pregnancies. The Alexander Technique has allowed me to think about my head and neck. I think about my head and neck when I'm stressed with my children. I keep thinking of returning to centre.'
Helen, pregnant with fourth child

3 | Use in Pregnancy

Introduction

There are many factors that affect your use in pregnancy, the most obvious being the extra weight you will be carrying. The average weight gain is 12kg, of which nearly half is made up of the baby, placenta, amniotic fluid and the uterus, and the rest comes from the increased size of the breasts, increase in body fluids and fat.

Many women, particularly those pregnant with their first baby, tend to stick out their stomachs as soon as they are pregnant. Unfortunately this throws the lumbar curve of the spine forwards and weakens the support provided by the lower back. Many women also focus attention towards their belly, sometimes cradling their 'bump' with their hands. This almost constant attention to the growing belly means that the pregnant woman slumps forwards from the upper back which increases the downwards pull of this additional weight in front.

Added to these factors is the ligament-softening effect of the hormone progesterone (see page 57). The function of ligaments is to hold joints securely and give postural stability but as they soften the skeletal structure becomes less secure, at a time when the extra weight is already putting an increased demand on the body. This makes it far easier for the body to be pulled out of shape.

'It's just the most miraculous thing you can imagine to create a new life and you want to look pregnant even when nobody knows that you are . . . this sticking the stomach out is a huge temptation and I remember I used to feel slightly cheated "being back in my back" instead of sticking my stomach out like other pregnant women I knew.' *Monique*

Misuse in Pregnancy

In four-legged animals the weight of pregnancy is distributed over four legs, but in humans all the extra weight (the baby, the uterus and the breasts) is carried at the front of the body. Because there is more weight in front there is an increased tendency for the body to fall forwards. The muscles at the back of the body therefore have to work more to maintain the balance. From an Alexander perspective, misuse is when this increased muscular activity is concentrated in specific areas.

The way in which a pregnant woman compensates for the increased imbalance will reflect her habitual misuse. If she has a tendency to an over-tense posture, she will pull her head and upper back backwards, by over-contracting the muscles of the lower back. The woman with a more collapsed posture will give up all attempt to retain her uprightness. In both cases the deep muscles in the pelvis and the muscles of the legs have to work extremely hard to maintain the balance, and there will be excessive tension in the joints, which will restrict their range of movement. The ligaments are also put under a lot of strain, because instead of doing their normal job – which is to make the joints more stable – they have to do a great deal of the work of supporting the body (which *should* be done by the muscles).

Unfortunately, instead of stabilizing the balance, this way of compensating creates a vicious circle of misuse. In both the over-tense posture and the collapsed posture, the lower back is allowed to curve forwards excessively, which throws the weight of the baby even more forwards. The body then has to further compensate by contracting muscles in an attempt to bring the centre of gravity back. And so it goes on, made worse by the fact that the baby meanwhile is increasing in size. This gives us the commonly accepted image of the pregnant woman having a very hollow back with the pregnancy carried far out in front. Some pregnancy books even suggest this is a physiologically natural aspect of pregnancy!

Good Use in Pregnancy

Maintaining good use in pregnancy is basically the same as when you are not pregnant. The muscles that keep the body upright need to work slightly more to counteract the 'pull' of the extra weight at the front. The important factor for good use is that this increased muscular activity needs to be equally distributed throughout the back of the body – not in specific areas. If we use ourselves in this way, the extra work that the muscles have to do can have a beneficial effect, as it is 'exercising' them.

As always we promote this good use by inhibiting and directing. Some Alexander teachers use the expression 'being in your back', which reminds

LEFT: *With Alexander directions the baby is effortlessly carried close to the mother's spine.*

RIGHT: *The posture usually adopted by pregnant women – which throws the baby forward and arches the back – can invite a host of problems.*

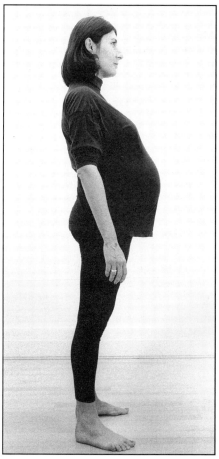

you to focus on your primary control, and encourages your weight to shift back towards the heels. We all know that when we are carrying a heavy object with both hands in front of us, the closer to the body we carry it the easier it is. We would not carry it far forwards on outstretched arms. We suggest that, in addition to the primary Alexander instructions, you think of the baby lying as close to the spine as possible and being cradled in your pelvis. Some women find a visual image helps this thinking. Imagine that your baby is in a shawl tied on to the spine, in much the same way as an African woman uses a shawl to hold the baby close to her body. Many women, maybe even subconsciously, have an image of the baby tilting precariously away from the body, probably because this is what we often see. You will find that purely thinking of the baby being snugly contained next to your spine will make it easier to maintain good use.

The Technique offers pregnant women a real choice in how they use their bodies to cope with the extra stress put on their spines by the weight of the baby. You don't have to suffer all the posturally related problems – you can enjoy your pregnancy! Having choice can also help how you feel about the pregnancy. It is possible to feel out of control, because the growing baby, plus the changes in the body, have a definite unstoppable momentum of their own. It can feel as if all this is going on in spite of you! Regaining choice (or experiencing that you have choice) re-establishes a sense of being in control.

'The only problem with carrying the baby well was that because nobody is accustomed to it, I had a lot of people tell me that I was having a small baby, which was rather disconcerting. Because I didn't stick out and I didn't have ultrasound I got everyone saying 6 pounds maximum. In fact Serena was 8 pounds. I had such a small bump because I was so much more "in my back", than many pregnant women who like to "show the world" their baby.' *Monique*

'There has been a fundamental change in my thinking since attending Alexander Technique classes. In the past when I got a pain in my back or my hips I'd immediately think: "I should see someone to get it fixed up." Now I think: "What am I doing incorrectly?" I relax my jaw, neck, shoulder muscles, try a different position. I am learning to be more aware of my body and the way habitual body positions can lead to muscle stress. It really feels like I am beginning to notice my body much more.' *Linley*

'I feel so much lighter after the Alexander classes. I feel as if I weigh a lot less.'
Sophie

Your Body in Pregnancy

Here we shall look at some very basic female anatomy and explore some of the changes that occur during pregnancy. We believe that having an understanding of this can positively affect your use.

One of the most important changes is caused by the release of a hormone called progesterone. This has the effect of softening all the soft tissues, i.e. the muscles, ligaments and tendons, making them more elastic and able to stretch.The purpose of this is to relax the ligaments securing the pelvic joints, thereby increasing the capacity of the pelvis, and to soften the pelvic floor muscles for the birth of the baby. However, not only do the joints in the pelvis become looser, but all the ligaments throughout the entire body become softened. This weakens certain structures of support, for example the spinal column, the sacroiliac joint, and the arches of the feet, which causes discomfort in pregnancy and can lead to long-term damage. Later in the book we will be looking at how better use can help prevent this.

There are two important groups of muscles in your body that come under great strain during pregnancy and childbirth and which should be given utmost priority. These are your *pelvic floor muscles* and your *abdominal muscles*. In the Alexander Technique we think of our musculature as a kind of 'body suit', rather like a diver's wet suit. Although there are separate muscles, they overlap and interweave with each other, making up the overall fabric of this suit, and functionally they act as a whole. The pelvic floor is the part of the suit that covers the bottom of the pelvis, running between the legs, and the abdominal muscles cover the front. In this section we will describe these muscles, the special demands put on them during pregnancy and how the Alexander Technique can help you maintain them in a healthy condition.

The Uterus

The uterus lies in the pelvis, surmounted by the ovaries and fallopian tubes, and with the bladder in front and the rectum behind. It is a hollow muscular organ which is shaped like, and is the approximate size of, a pear, weighing around 60g. It is secured by strong ligaments that attach to the sacrum, the inside of the pelvis, and the vulva. When a non-pregnant woman is standing upright the uterus lies almost horizontally. During pregnancy, however, the position changes so that by term it is almost vertical, having grown to a length of 30cm, and a weight of 1kg.

LEFT: *The uterus before pregnancy*

RIGHT: *The uterus and ligaments during pregnancy*

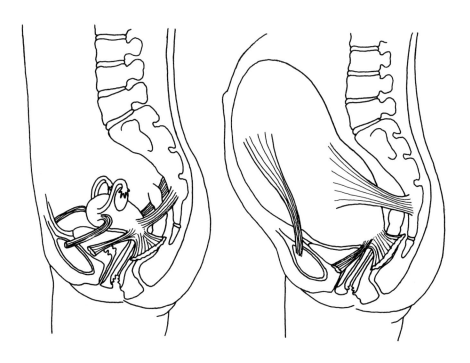

There are three layers in the uterus. The inner layer of muscle fibres are circular and are most plentiful in the lower part of the uterus; this allows the lower segment to stretch and the cervix to open. In the middle layer the fibres run obliquely around the uterus, crossing and recrossing each other in a figure of eight. They contract and retract during labour, playing a major role in 'pulling up' the cervix, and also control bleeding after the placenta separates. The outer layer of fibres runs longitudinally from the cervix to the top of the uterus, and is mainly used in the second stage of labour, contracting and retracting to shorten the uterus and expel the baby.

The Pelvis

The pelvis is like a strong bony basin which contains and protects the reproductive organs, the bladder, the rectum and the intestines. Together with the spine, the pelvis supports the upper body and transmits its weight into the legs. It acts as a major shock absorber of weight thrust in movement. The pelvis is the origin of many muscles which insert into the trunk, arms and legs. The pelvic joints are protected by strong ligaments and fibrous tissue to keep them in place and allow only a small range of movement. This is necessary to make the pelvis stable enough to perform its supportive functions.

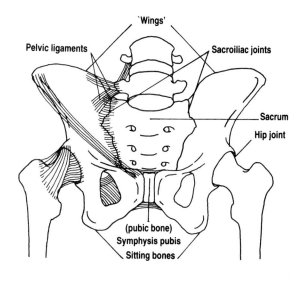

The upper rims of the pelvis are the bony crests at either side, usually referred to as our hips. If you put your hands on these rims and follow them round to the back you come to the sacrum. At the bottom of the pelvis are two bones commonly called sitting bones, because the weight of the body falls on to them when we are sitting. Tuck your upturned hands under the buttocks while sitting, and you will feel these bones, like two rockers on which the torso pivots. To locate your pubic bone, squat down and explore the lower side of the pubic arch, which extends down from the pubic bone as far as your sitting bones. You can feel this joint moving in pregnancy if you put your fingers on it while you move from one leg to the other.

The lower part of the pelvis, or the true pelvis, is what is important because this is the bony structure through which the baby must pass. It is rather like a slightly curved cylinder or funnel. At the top, the inlet or 'brim' is the oval-shaped entrance and at the bottom is the pelvic outlet, through which the baby passes as it is born. The cavity is the curved passageway which runs in between the inlet and the outlet.

The muscles of the pelvic floor form a figure of eight around the three openings (the urethra, the vagina and the anus). These muscles strengthen and support the sphincters and the inner passages and are anchored into the perineal body.

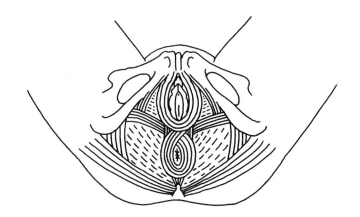

The Pelvic Floor

Although the pelvic floor is crucial to our health and well-being, there is a general lack of awareness of what it is, and what it does. The pelvic floor is like a hammock which runs from the pubic bone at the front to the sacrum and coccyx at the back. It is made up of muscles, ligaments and connective tissue which surround the pelvic organs and as the name suggests form the floor of the pelvis.

The pelvic floor supports the pelvic organs (the bladder, uterus, and bowel) and provides the sphincter control of the vagina, the urethra and the rectum which pass through it. It enables the body to withstand the changes in pressure within the pelvic and abdominal cavity during activities such as laughing, coughing, sneezing, defecation, and pushing during the second stage of labour. It is also designed to release sufficiently to let the full-term baby pass through comfortably. The pelvic floor is, in fact, perfectly designed for easy childbirth.

It is important that the pelvic floor has a healthy muscle tone and elasticity. If it is allowed to become slack, a range of distressing urogenital problems may occur. There can be more general symptoms – such as aches in the pelvic region and fatigue and a loss of feeling during intercourse – or more specifically symptoms such as prolapse of the uterus and urinary stress incontinence. Factors that contribute to these problems include childbearing, decreasing hormone levels after the menopause, and age.

Pelvic floor problems are very common and on the whole the medical profession tends to accept them as inevitable. However, in the 1960s Dr Arnold Kegel, an American neurologist and gynaecologist working with new mothers with incontinence problems, devised a set of preventive and corrective exercises that involved contracting and relaxing the pelvic floor. The exercises were phenomenally successful, and replaced surgical correction as a treatment in his clinic; they are now routinely taught in antenatal lessons worldwide.

From further research he found that the origin of many of these problems was not that the pelvic floor was too lax but that it was chronically too tight and therefore was not able to function properly. By teaching his patients to release excessive tension in their pelvic floors they were able to get a healthy muscle tone, and subsequently improved functioning. A side benefit of Dr Kegel's work was that women reported a vast improvement in their sexual response, some previously non-orgasmic women having orgasms.

Use and the pelvic floor

The pelvic floor is a vital component of our overall good use. When there is a good head/neck/back relationship (when the muscles of the front and back of the body are stretching in a dynamic way) then the pelvic floor will work as integral part of the overall 'suit of musculature' and will have a healthy muscle tone Unfortunately, most people hold on too tightly in the pelvic floor area. There may be several reasons for this: women being told to keep their knees together because it 'looks nicer'; being told to 'tuck your bottom under' so it does not stick out; and perhaps because of the fear of not being able to control bladder and bowel functions.

This chronically held tension in the pelvic floor adversely affects overall use. Because of the physical proximity of the muscles of the pelvic floor, the deep pelvic muscles, the buttocks and the inner thighs, tension in one set of muscles will affect the amount of tension in others. Thus it is vital that we learn how to consciously direct these muscles to release, as then the other sets of muscles will also release.

We achieve this using the Alexander Technique by working with the fourth 'direction': to 'let the knees go forward and away'. The effect of this is to release the excessive muscle tension in the inner thighs that pulls the knees together. When the inner thighs release, the pelvic floor, the buttocks and the deep pelvic muscles also release. This direction is particularly important for pregnant women for whom it is vital that they can release their pelvic floors.

The pelvic floor in pregnancy and birth

Good use will on its own encourage healthy tone in the pelvic floor but it is also crucial that you practise pelvic floor exercises, because these muscles are not adequately exercised during any other activity (except perhaps intercourse). During pregnancy the weight of the growing uterus puts increasing pressure on the pelvic floor, which can cause the muscles to become progressively slacker. It is therefore very important to have good muscle tone so that they can perform their supportive role for the pelvic organs.

Varicose veins in the vulva and haemorrhoids, which are both caused by blood congesting in the perineum as well as constipation, are common problems in pregnancy. The increased muscular activity during pelvic floor exercises improves circulation, stimulates bowel movement and helps eliminate these problems.

Learning to release the knees forwards and away, and practising pelvic floor exercises, is a vital preparation for labour. During delivery the pelvic floor ceases its supportive function and completely releases to allow the baby through. It stretches and thins out, rather like a sweater's neckline as you push your head through it. During the last few weeks of the pregnancy, hormones make the muscles softer and more elastic to allow this to happen.

When muscles are healthy and elastic, with a good blood supply, they will survive the enormous stretch during delivery and regenerate more quickly afterwards. Being familiar with the sensations of your pelvic floor will make it a lot easier for you to inhibit the desire to contract and resist the powerful sensations in the second stage of labour, allowing your muscles to open up. Being able to release your pelvic floor muscles also makes vaginal examinations much easier; you can decide to respond with a releasing and opening towards the touch of the midwife or doctor.

Pelvic floor exercises

Pelvic floor exercises need to be practised by all women, whether mothers or not, on a daily basis, throughout their life. Muscle fibres are like elastic fibres, but unlike the manufactured kind they become more elastic with careful and repeated contraction and relaxation.

For these exercises you need to isolate the action of pelvic floor muscles as much as possible. Do be careful that you do not tighten the abdominals, the buttocks, and the muscles of the inner thighs rather than the pelvic floor. This is easily done at first. To avoid this, try the exercises in a monkey, or a lunge, because in these positions your inner thighs and buttock muscles are releasing, and it is much easier to have an awareness of the pelvic floor.

Perhaps surprisingly, there exists a direct relationship between the muscles of the jaw and mouth and those of the pelvic floor. It is quite easy to feel this. Try pursing your lips tightly and notice your pelvic floor tightening in response. Slowly soften your lips and notice the gradual release of the pelvic floor. Because of this intimate relationship, do keep your face as soft as possible, while performing the following exercise.

PELVIC FLOOR EXERCISE INSTRUCTIONS

Contract the pelvic floor muscles, concentrating on the muscles of the vaginal sphincter. Think high up in your vagina, because you need to tighten not only the muscles of the sphincter, but also the fibres that blend into the walls of the birth canal which are higher up inside. Hold for two or three seconds and then release. Pay attention to the feeling of release you have achieved, and then consciously slacken the muscles a little more. Always finish with a contraction so that the pelvic floor resumes its supportive muscular tone.

Once you have mastered the basic contraction and release exercise, imagine that your pelvic floor is a lift, and draw up the muscles to take you, floor by floor, to the fifth floor. When you are there, you can then descend, again floor by floor, reaching the 'ground floor', then allow the muscles to release even more until you reach the 'basement'. Make sure that you always finish with the lift at the ground floor, so that once again the muscles are performing their supportive function.

Do not try to do too many of these exercises at once, or try holding for prolonged periods, as this can weaken and damage the muscles. Practise only for as long as you can keeping the same strength of muscle contraction. Stop when you feel the contractions weaken. Remember, it is better to do a few exercises whenever you happen to remember them, rather than go for a long session, which strains the muscles.

The abdominal muscles are intermeshed to a high degree and therefore muscular activity can never be completely isolated to one set of muscles.

Abdominal Muscles

For most women the major concern about their abdominal muscles is their appearance. The desirable image presented through fashion and many exercise regimes is of a flat tummy, and women are often encouraged to hold their stomach in or try to disguise it under their clothes. Feeling good about our looks is of course necessary, but in reality the major importance of the abdominal muscles for a woman's well-being is how well they are performing their vital functions of assisting in breathing, posture and movement, and supporting the abdominal contents. If every woman thought of her abdominal muscles from this perspective she would in fact both look and feel much better. In childbearing, healthy abdominal muscles support the baby better, assist in an easier delivery and will recover their pre-pregnant state more easily.

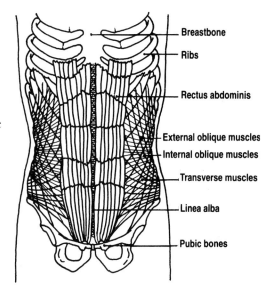

- Breastbone
- Ribs
- Rectus abdominis
- External oblique muscles
- Internal oblique muscles
- Transverse muscles
- Linea alba
- Pubic bones

The abdominal muscles are the part of the body's suit of musculature which runs from the pubic bone of the pelvis up to the breastbone and ribcage, and round to the sides attaching to the pelvic ridge. (It is a good idea to locate these bones for yourself so that you have a clearer picture of the area they cover.) They form a firm but elastic wall which helps to keep the abdominal and pelvic organs in position (in pregnancy this includes the uterus and baby), making certain movements possible and playing a vital role in your use, assisting in breathing, talking, singing, shouting, laughing and all expulsive acts such as coughing, sneezing, vomiting, urination and defecation, as well as in the expulsion of the baby in the second stage of labour.

Use and the abdominal muscles

A surprising number of people habitually over-tense the abdominal muscles. This can be the result of excessive stress in their lives, which often seems to focus in the stomach area, or it can be because they pull their tummies in, trying to achieve a flat stomach. Many people also think – wrongly – that they need to hold on with their abdominal muscles to support the spine, or help a back problem. In pregnancy this becomes impossible anyway.

Over-tense abdominal muscles are particularly harmful to your use because they pull the spine forwards from the upper back. The muscles of the back then over-contract to keep you upright and the whole spine is pulled out of alignment. Another effect of over-tense abdominals is that the space in the abdominal cavity is diminished, which cramps the organs and restricts blood and nerve supply, and the rhythmic movement necessary for their functioning. In some people, however, the abdominals can be too lax, and this can also adversely affect overall use.

Both over-tense muscles and muscles that are too lax are an indication of poor use and are contrary to Alexander thinking. In the Alexander Technique we achieve a healthy tone in the abdominal muscles by maintaining a good head/neck/back relationship, and thinking long through the abdominals in an upward direction. We are looking for a 'lengthening' of the spine, i.e. a reduction in the curves, and an increase in stature. When this happens we get a balanced working of the muscles of the front of the trunk with those of the back – the muscles that were over-tense will release, and those that were too lax will be brought into play and be energized.

'That habit of mine of holding on with my tummy muscles has had to go because they are so stretched. It seems physically impossible.' *Sarah*

'I realize now how much I have always used my abdominal muscles to move and to bend and to lift myself up. Since I have become pregnant I have found that I have to find other ways of moving.' *Jenny*

Abdominal muscles in pregnancy

The state of your abdominal muscles and the changes that they have to go through are of major concern during pregnancy and in the recovery period afterwards. To be able to accommodate the size of the pregnant uterus the abdominal muscles have to stretch by an incredible amount. This becomes particularly noticeable towards the end of the pregnancy when the navel becomes so stretched that it flattens out and stretch marks appear on the skin. However, if you look after these muscles at this time and after the birth they are capable of returning to their pre-pregnant state.

It is particularly important that these muscles have a healthy tone while you are pregnant because they are being called on to help support the weight of the uterus and baby. The closer the abdominals can hold the baby to your spine, the less forwards 'pull' there is on your spine, and the less your lumbar spine gets pulled out of shape. If your muscles are weak, the weight of the baby spills forwards, and pulls your lower back with it. It is often in second and subsequent pregnancies, where the muscles have not regained their former strength and are unable to support the baby snugly into the body, that women start to suffer back problems.

To minimize damage to these muscles when they are already stretched to their limit, you are advised to avoid activities that further stretch and possibly damage them. Take extra care while lifting, a very common activity if you already have small children, and getting out of bed. (See page 70.)

The recti muscles (the vertical ones) are under the most strain. They are separated into two halves which are joined at a central 'seam line' called the linea alba. In many women this is quite visible in later pregnancy when it turns a darker colour. Sometimes this seam separates, either during pregnancy or in the labour, in much the same way as a seam in a garment can come apart when put under too much stress. It is possible to rehabilitate this muscle once the baby has been born using specific exercises. (See *Essential Exercises for the Childbearing Year* by Elizabeth Noble.)

Exercises for toning the abdominal muscles

It is important to develop a healthy muscle tone before (if possible) and during the pregnancy. Supple and elastic abdominal muscles can stretch more easily and support the pregnancy better, assist in an easier birth and contract back into shape more quickly after the baby is born.

Healthy muscle tone, as we have seen, is dependent on overall use. In the Alexander Technique we never think of one set of muscles working in isolation from the rest, and the way your abdominal muscles work is dependent on the way the whole body is used. The way that you are taught to use yourself in Alexander lessons – to keep the neck free and allow the back to lengthen and move as a whole, and using movements such as monkey, squatting and lunging for your everyday activities – promotes good tone in these muscles.

However, our normal everyday activities may not include the whole range of movements required to tone up the abdominals, particularly if we lead a sedentary lifestyle, with all its activity-saving conveniences. Therefore, we recommend that you practise some abdominal exercises during this time when extra demand is being put on them.

Details of commonly taught exercises can be found in a number of general books on pregnancy and childbirth (see the list of further reading on page 157). However, there are some exercises that we strongly advise you against. These include all kinds of 'sit-ups' with straight legs, and straight leg raises with both legs extended, both of which can cause back strain and unnatural ligament and nerve elongation, weakening the lower back.

Some exercises are safe, however, and these can usually be practised throughout pregnancy. A note of caution: if any of the exercises cause pain or discomfort you should consult your midwife or doctor. Remember that in the later stages of pregnancy, exercises done lying on your back may cause restrictions in the blood flow to both you and your baby as the weight of the uterus falls on to the main blood supply. If there are any signs of dizziness, shortness of breath or discomfort, stop and change position. These exercises can also be used for getting back into shape after the baby is born

The exercises should not be practised as a quick routine but with direction and conscious control. Breathing is a very important consideration in any kind of activity. Move slowly and gently enough to allow smooth and continuous breathing. Do only a few of each at one go, and always finish with an Alexander resting position. *It is not how many times, how quickly or how strenuously you do them that counts – it is how well you do them that makes them really effective.* We also advise you, if possible, to ask your Alexander teacher to take you through these exercises to help you maintain your directions while doing them and to make sure that you are not harming yourself.

Two beneficial abdominal exercises that we recommend are both done in semi-supine. The first is to lie and gently rock the legs from side to side; in the second, one leg at a time is gently extended in a sliding motion and then returned to the bent-knee position. Hip-hitches or tail-wagging on all fours is another well known and safe exercise.

4 Everyday Activities During Pregnancy

Maintaining good use is a constant balancing act, and in pregnancy you have to be particularly careful, especially with the increased weight of the baby pulling you forward. In the following everyday activities, we give you a few pointers to good use.

Standing

The majority of people, if they stand for any length of time, tend to stiffen and become fixed, particularly in the lower back and the legs. It is in fact quite a tiring activity. As every pregnant woman knows, carrying the extra weight of the baby can make standing even for a short time exhausting. Another unpleasant consequence is that you may feel faint, and indeed may faint. The blood from the legs is pumped back to the heart by the movement of the muscles in the legs. The faintness is caused by the fall in blood pressure which occurs as the blood pools in the legs because there is no movement in the muscles to pump the blood back.

The most important advice we can give is first and foremost to avoid standing for long periods wherever possible. It puts a lot of strain on your body and the less unnecessary stress you can give yourself the better. Having said this, of course in real life there are situations where it is unavoidable. Here are some general hints about standing which will help you both while pregnant and in your everyday life afterwards.

A very common habit of faulty use in standing is to stand with more weight over the balls of the feet, and the joints in the legs locked. It is therefore worth reminding you that to counteract this tendency you need to give your Alexander directions so that your weight shifts back towards the heels and is evenly distributed through the front and the back of the feet.

Some women find that standing with the feet wide apart, which gives a broader base, can seem more stable, but this is in fact deceptive. With the feet wide apart there is no firm base of support directly underneath the torso. As a result the whole trunk sags and 'drops down between the legs'. With this stance it is also very easy to 'rigidify' or fix in the legs and this interferes with freedom of movement. It is preferable to stand with the feet directly below the hips and the toes pointing out at a slight angle, so that the weight of your torso is transmitted directly through your legs into the ground.

Another very common habit is to stand with all the weight on one leg, tilting the pelvis and dropping down into the hip, which twists the spine. A practical alternative – which looks both relaxed and poised – is to stand with one foot slightly behind the other. Many of Alexander's students were performers who had to stand for a long time and Alexander used to teach them to stand like this. You can slide one foot back an inch or two and let the weight rest mainly on the rear foot. By sliding one foot back, rather than putting one foot in front you are less likely to sink down into your hips. This gives you a freer base with more mobility and springiness. Take care to alternate this stance at intervals, by changing the foot that is behind because even in this position it is possible for your muscles to fix.

Even if you are thinking about maintaining your good use, it is very easy for your muscles to stiffen when you are not moving, because the limited number of muscles and ligaments supporting you are under a constant strain. The following are movements that will make standing less tiring.

Standing in a very slight monkey (see pages 34–6) allows the muscles of the lower back to stretch out. Where possible, make use of any available support. You can lean your bottom (or whole back) against a wall, or you could lean on a table, allowing your hands to share the weight. Take special care to inhibit the temptation to slump against the support you use.

Another possibility in monkey is to gently rock from one leg to the other. This is advantageous because it alternates the weight going through the pelvic ligaments. You can rock from side to side while standing with your feet parallel, or you can slide one foot back an inch or two then rock backwards and forwards. Alternatively you can walk on the spot, without actually taking your toes off the ground. Go up on your toes on one foot and then up on the other. Directing your knee forwards, let the heel 'peel' off the floor, so that the weight goes out over the toes. Take care to keep the length in the back – it will help if you think of staying back over the supporting foot while moving the other. This is useful if you feel faint as it exercises the calf muscles which have a strong pumping action helping the return of the blood to the heart. (It is also, alas, a movement that can easily trigger habitual misuse, so ask your Alexander teacher to take you through it.)

Walking

We can often recognize someone by the way they walk just as easily as we would recognize their face. They may bounce up and down on the balls of their feet, sink down into their knees with each step or sway their hips, or shoulders. These are superfluous movements making walking less efficient, and are all too often an expression of their particular misuse of themselves.

Perhaps the most common misuse in walking is that, because the primary control is not operating well, as one leg moves forwards the pelvis follows, pulling the upper body with it. The head is pulled back and down and the weight of the upper body falls heavily downwards into the front leg at every step, thus compressing all the joints in the legs, particularly the hips, and stopping them moving freely.

Walking with good use depends specifically on maintaining your primary control and most importantly remembering that the movement of the legs is secondary to the movement of the integrated unit of the head, neck and back. During walking, the weight of the body has to balance on the column of support created by one leg, while the other leg swings forwards. In order to release tension and discourage heaviness in the joints, you need to think of letting the head go forwards and upwards and allow that to start the movement. This releases the weight of the body off the legs, allowing them to move more freely. As you walk forwards you will be continuing to direct up, thereby staying light, and instead of falling heavily downwards on to the leading leg, you are 'falling' upwards. Try standing on one leg, and if you think of your body lengthening upwards you will find it much easier to maintain your balance than if you collapse on to your supporting leg.

Being able to walk with good use is extremely important when you are pregnant. We are all used to seeing the characteristic side-to-side 'waddle' in pregnant women. Some women may unconsciously adopt this as a way of walking in the same way that people conform to other peer group postures like the 'adolescent slump' or the 'macho male' swagger, but it is more usually the effect of poor use. With poor use, the weight of the pregnancy increases the tendency to fall downwards into the front leg. The freedom of movement in the hip joints becomes so restricted that the legs are effectively locked on to the body. With each step the front leg pulls the upper body from side to side, giving us the 'waddle' or rocking side to side. Walking in this way increases the forwards curvature of the lumbar spine, and puts a great deal of stress on the muscles and ligaments of the lower back.

'I believe that your "hands on" and advice helped me not to walk like a duck, or is it waddle like a duck.' *Francine*

Fortunately, as your general use improves with Alexander lessons you will be able to walk with a feeling of lightness and poise, even while heavily pregnant. Your teacher can take you through walking as part of your lessons, looking at what is involved in taking a step and keeping your directions while you walk.

Sleeping

A common question asked of Alexander teachers is whether there are any recommended sleeping positions. It is not really helpful to recommend a position, because once you are asleep you are no longer in conscious control. It is most likely that your sleeping posture will reflect your habitual use, and the state you were in when you went to bed. It is more helpful to reduce the amount of unnecessary tension in the body so that the positions you naturally adopt while asleep are more relaxed. If you find that you tend to sleep in a very tense and contracted position, it is worth doing semi-supine (or in the latter stage of pregnancy one of the alternative resting positions) for ten to fifteen minutes immediately before going to sleep (see pages 46–50). This usually ensures a more relaxed night's sleep.

As the baby grows, most women find it harder and harder to find a comfortable sleeping position. There is no easy solution, except to suggest that you give your body as much support as possible. Most helpful seems to be a pillow between your legs, and, if you are lying on your side, one to support the baby. This may mean that you have so many pillows there is barely room for your partner, but it is the best way to get the rest you need!

Getting Out of Bed

As you get bigger in size you will find that it gets progressively more difficult to manoeuvre your body out of bed. Sitting straight up (as in a 'sit-up') puts too much strain on the abdominal muscles and can lead to separation of the rectus muscles. Instead, the safest (and in the later stages the easiest) way to get up is to first of all roll on to your side, bend both knees and then use the arms to lever your upper body upright. You can then swing your legs over the side of the bed. Do be careful to keep the head, neck and back in one piece, as twisting from the waist will put unnecessary pressure on the sacroiliac joint. The ligaments are at their most relaxed after a night's sleep, so it is important that you are careful not to strain them.

If your back feels stiff when you wake up, it is a good idea to do some gentle warm-up exercises before you get out of bed. While lying on your back, bend your knees and gently let the legs rock from side to side. This will get the muscles moving so that you won't strain them by going into weight-bearing movement straightaway.

Lifting

Lifting is looked at in detail in the section on caring for the baby (see pages 140–2), but it is important to mention it here because you need to be especially careful about lifting while you are pregnant. Your ligaments and joints are more vulnerable because of the effect of progesterone, you are already carrying the extra weight of the baby, and your abdominals are already weakened because they are stretched to their limit. You should avoid lifting wherever possible. Many women manage in their first pregnancy to avoid back problems; it is with the second and subsequent pregnancies, where they also have to cope with other children, that most harm is done to their backs.

If you pick something up by bending at the waist and keeping your legs straight you are putting a dangerous amount of strain on your back. Fortunately there is a short-term protective reflex mechanism whereby the breath is held, causing the throat, the pelvic floor and abdominal muscles to contract thereby bracing the body and spreading some of the strain of the weight of the object into the pelvis. This is an incorrect way to lift, and it is out of the question if you are pregnant because of the stress it puts on the abdominals and the pelvic floor. It also raises the blood pressure.

To lift safely and effectively, bend your knees and incline your back *slightly* forwards in one piece, i.e. go into a monkey. The legs provide a strong base, the height of which is adjustable by bending at the hips, knees and ankles. This provides a lever system which spreads the load evenly rather than the arms, shoulders and lower back taking all the strain. If you learn to lift correctly while you are pregnant, as well as preventing damage to your body you will also be establishing good habits as preparation for all the lifting you will be doing after the baby is born.

Relaxation

While you are pregnant it is extremely important that you take rests. For this we encourage you to use an Alexander resting position. In early pregnancy you can use semi-supine (see pages 46–50), and in later pregnancy either lie on your side supported by cushions or sit backwards on a chair. Resting in one of these positions and spending time inhibiting and directing releases unnecessary muscular tension in your body and encourages the functioning of the primary control. It is far better than lying down on a bed and having a catnap, when you would probably maintain your usual muscular tension patterns. If it helps you to relax, you can listen to music. (Of course most women need a lot more sleep when they are pregnant, so try to get some proper sleep during the day, as well.)

This Alexander 'habit' of giving yourself time to slow down and centre on your body is invaluable, whether you are pregnant or not. It is probably one of the most effective forms of 'relaxation' available. It gives you a time where you can truly inhibit excessive nervous tension and access a deep state of stillness. When you are giving birth you need to be able to focus inwards, and go into a quiet state inside, in order to be able to tune into your body's needs and stay calm and centred.

Given the lifestyles that most of us lead it is extremely important that you practise this throughout the pregnancy, so that by the time you go into labour you can access this state with ease. Sheila Kitzinger uses the Quaker term 'centring down', which is an apt description.

Lying on Your Side

To lie on your side and get the maximum support for your back you need a higher support for your head than when lying on your back. You can use books or a firm pillow. Your knees should be slightly bent with the uppermost knee more so, and placed in front of the other one. You will need to place a pillow or two close to you so that you can rest your tummy and the upper knee on them.

In this position you can still promote a good head/neck/back relationship, by paying special attention to the contact points on the floor: the head, the upper back and the pelvis.

Lying on side.

'Posture of a child'

This position (*above*) is very restful for the back, letting it widen and allowing free breathing. A tonic for a tired lower back, it is a good way of preserving energy and staying calm in the early part of labour.

Sitting astride a chair

This is very comfortable for resting and for when you have to sit for long periods (*right*). It gives you a chance to work your Alexander directions and on releasing the muscles of the inner thigh and pelvic floor. You can either lean on cushions or sit more upright, depending on whether you want a resting position or to be more active and alert. It gives you many of the advantages of squatting, but it is not so tiring.

5 Breathing in Pregnancy

Introduction

Breathing is the most basic of all our vital functions, and one of the most magical moments you can experience is watching a newborn baby take its first breath. Breathing well gives us better general health and well-being; it ensures healthy functioning not only of the heart and lungs, but of all the systems of the body. Full and rhythmic breathing makes us calmer and gives us emotional stability. Breathing gives us life and is the key with which you can connect into your inner self.

The automatic process of breathing is controlled by the respiratory centres of the brain. It is a highly sensitive mechanism which is designed to change in response to our varying circumstances. Different physical activities require different rates and rhythms of breathing. Our breathing changes in response to our state of health, our mental and emotional states, and in response to the need for breath when using the voice. When the breathing muscles are working freely, the breathing mechanism can attune to the activity in hand and thus ensure an adequate supply of oxygen and removal of carbon dioxide at all times.

The Alexander Technique and Breathing

As a result of his overall co-ordination and good use, Alexander had remarkable control of his breathing mechanism, and he became known as 'the breathing man'. In his early days of teaching he placed a lot of emphasis on teaching correct breathing. He realized that how a person breathes is dependent on their general use, and that having a good head/neck/back relationship is of primary importance. This ensures that the spine provides good support for the ribcage, and for the muscles

'. . . it is a scientific fact that all "physical" tension tends to cause thoracic (chest) rigidity and breathlessness' *F.M. Alexander*

involved in breathing that are attached to it, and that both the ribcage and the breathing muscles are able to move freely.

By giving directions we release all the muscles that are attached to the spine. The discs between each of the bones of the spine are no longer being compressed, and are able to expand, and this creates further lengthening of the spine. The extra length means that there is more space between the ribs at their attachment to the spine. This allows freer and increased movement (both expansion and contraction, the contraction being equally important) in the ribcage, and this movement has the effect of giving a gentle 'massage' to all the muscles involved in breathing, which makes them release. Consequently there is not only a lengthening of the spine, but also an increase in the circumference of the whole of the ribcage, and in fact the whole torso. In Alexander terms, a lengthening and widening of the back occurs.

Alexander found that poor breathing was a result of excessive muscular tension in any part of the body, because it interfered with the free movement of these breathing muscles. Muscular tension that affected the lengthening of the spine, and the head/neck/back relationship, was the most detrimental.

As you breathe out, the diaphragm relaxes and moves upwards. The abdominal muscles contract and assist the rib muscles in their action of bringing the ribcage in and down again. The chest cavity is now narrowed in all directions which expels the air from the lungs. This is like closing a pair of bellows.

As you breathe in, the diaphragm contracts – it flattens and lowers, and the abdominals relax. The rib muscles lift the ribs upwards and outwards. In this way, the chest cavity is increased in all directions, a partial vacuum is created in the lungs, and the breath is drawn in. This is like opening a pair of bellows.

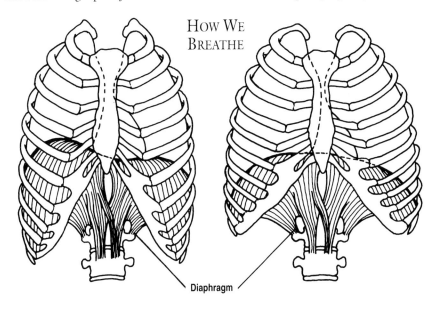

HOW WE BREATHE

Diaphragm

Typical tension patterns that affect breathing adversely often involve tension in the neck and shoulders, a rigid ribcage – either slumped or held high (often in a mistaken attempt at 'good posture') – and excessive tension in abdominals, the lower back muscles and the deep pelvic muscles.

These misuses lead to poor breathing habits, such as holding the breath, or gasping for air. People commonly hold the breath to concentrate, during movements which require great strength such as lifting, and in order not to feel unpleasant feelings or pain. 'Gasping' is a common habit which is easy to hear among media presenters and public speakers. We may not even be aware of these habits until we have unusual demands put on our breathing, for example if we use our voice in performance or while doing strenuous exercise. These habits not only give us an inadequate supply of oxygen, but also further harm our use.

Faulty breathing habits also interrupt the 'rhythmicity' of breathing. Although the rhythm of breathing can change – the depth or shallowness, or length of in-breath in relation to out-breath – it is important that there is an uninterrupted in-breath for out-breath, like the ebb and flow of tidal waves, to secure a regular exchange of air.

Perhaps surprisingly, many of these problems occur because we do not breathe out adequately. They can be corrected by working on improving our overall use and by learning how to breathe out properly. In normal breathing, exhaling should take almost twice as long as inhaling. Alexander devised an exercise specifically with this in mind called the 'whispered ah'.

The Whispered Ah

The whispered ah is an exercise to encourage the release of any tension in the musculature that is restricting the breathing, particularly in the jaw, throat and neck. The emphasis during the whispered ah is on the exhalation, not on the inhalation. If we can keep a good head/neck/back relationship as we breathe out fully, we set up the conditions that will allow a spontaneous in-breath to occur. It is therefore extremely effective for changing poor breathing habits and brings about an uninterrupted exchange of in-breath for out-breath.

WHISPERED AH INSTRUCTIONS

The first thing to remember before proceeding with the whispered ah is, as always, to give your directions to maintain a good head/neck/back relationship.

Start with your mouth closed, lips touching gently. Your tongue should be lying flat, with the tip placed behind the lower teeth, but not pushed against them. Try to think of something funny or pleasant to

 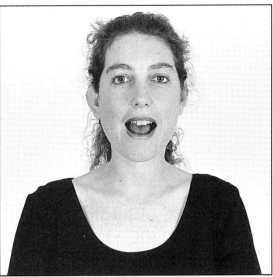

make you smile. A stage smile will not do; it has to be a real smile with the eyes, as this lifts the facial muscles and allows the jaw to move freely. It also enlivens and lifts the soft palate. Smiling in this way will open up space in your throat, preparing you for the next stage.

Now open the mouth by allowing the jaw to move forward and down – make sure you don't tip your head back. The tip of your tongue will still be behind your lower teeth and you should still be smiling and giving your directions.

You are now ready to breathe out, whispering 'ah', allowing the sound out through a very open throat. It is important here that you do *not* take a breath before breathing out. The out-breath should not in any way be forced, nor should it be like a resigned sigh accompanied by a collapse of the ribcage. Listening to the sound you produce is a good guide to how free and open your throat is and how well you are performing this procedure. It should be a smooth and 'open' sound. If, for example, you hear a guttural rasping sound or a glottal stop (a 'popping' sound before a vowel) you know that you are producing tension in your throat.

Close the mouth again as the out-breath comes to an end, and allow the air to come in through the nose. If you have kept your directions and your smile during the expiration, the air will enter the lungs as a reflex action as soon as you release your abdominal muscles and the ribcage. You do not have to make any extra effort to pull the air in, by gasping or sniffing. Check your directions and then repeat the procedure.

The whispered ah can usefully be practised every day of your life; it has far-reaching effects on your general health and well-being, and it is the basis for all good voice work.

You can practise the whispered ah with a partner or in front of a mirror, either sitting or standing. This helps you to keep the eyes alive and to keep the smile going. If you use a mirror, you will be able to observe if you are pulling down your chest in front or collapsing, or if you are lifting your shoulders and chest. You will also be able to see how open your mouth is, as you whisper the ah. People often think that they have opened the mouth quite wide, but when they take a look the teeth are only far enough apart to let a fingertip between them. The mouth needs to be more open than that, but do not force it open. You can also practise the whispered ah in semi-supine or in monkey.

Although we have given you instructions for this procedure, it is preferable that you learn it initially with the help of your teacher. The whispered ah may appear simple, but easy it is not. Before you have gained a more reliable sensory awareness it is very difficult to know for yourself whether you are doing it correctly.

'As I went into UCH with high blood pressure they said that if it didn't go down they would have to do a Caesarean, so I just sat there and did lots of whispered ahs. Within an hour the pressure was down from 105 to 95. I was quite surprised how I handled it. I had a choice as to how to respond when I heard the midwives talk about it. My husband sang Turkish nursery rhymes and talked to the baby – we all tried to stay calm.' *Paula*

The whispered ah and pelvic floor release

In normal healthy breathing the pelvic floor muscles release slightly on the in-breath and contract on the out-breath. However, in labour it is important to keep the pelvic floor as released as possible. Because of the relationship between tension in the jaw and around the mouth, and tension in the pelvic floor, the whispered ah is a very effective way of releasing the pelvic floor muscles. Even more effective is the following adaptation.

As you breathe out and whisper ah imagine that you are sending the air out through your pelvic floor. You should feel the pelvic floor muscles soften as the imagined breath permeates the whole area. You can do this at any time and in any position. Monkey and lunge are ideal.

'I am amazed how tension in one part of our body gets transmitted to another part. I've never thought that tension in my jaw could affect my vaginal muscles.' *Linley*

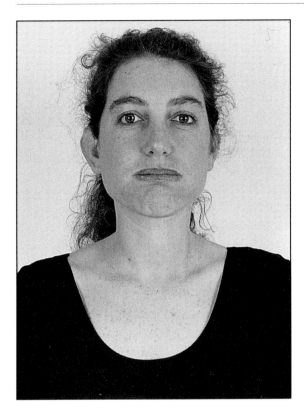
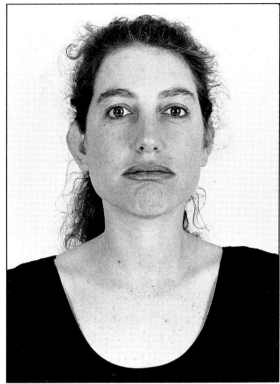

Puffy Cheek Breathing

This is another breathing exercise, used by Alexander teacher Refia Sacks. It is based on the whispered ah and gives you the same benefits, but it has the further advantage of heightening awareness of your lips and face, making it easier to release tension in this area and consequently in the pelvic floor.

Both puffy cheek breathing and whispered ah can be used to help you relax when you are having an internal examination. They can also be used in the pushing stage of labour.

LEFT: *Cheeks puffed out, mouth gently closed*

RIGHT: *Exhaling the air through soft, passive lips*

PUFFY CHEEK BREATHING INSTRUCTIONS

As with the whispered ah, the emphasis is on the out-breath. Puff the cheeks out by filling the mouth with air, so that the cheeks are expanded but not stretched tight. Let your lips be gently closed, teeth apart. Slowly blow the air out against the resistance of soft, passive lips, while keeping your cheeks puffed. When you have finished exhaling close your mouth and let the air come in again through the nose. Repeat this two or three times.

Breathing in Pregnancy

During your pregnancy it is vital that you are breathing well to provide the oxygen both for your own body's increased needs and for those of the growing baby. The common tension patterns that can occur as a result of carrying the baby with poor use, such as increased muscular tension in the lumbar spine and leaning backwards from the waist, can interfere with your breathing mechanism. If you are breathing well, this improves your circulation, and the health of your heart and lungs, and you will be less likely to suffer from breathlessness.

Breathlessness in the later stages of pregnancy is very common because there is simply less room for the diaphragm to descend. If the amount of room for your lungs to expand is already restricted because of tightness of the breathing muscles, breathlessness is much more likely. Right from the beginning of your pregnancy your Alexander teacher will show you how to allow a full expansion of the ribcage, especially at the back, so that you use the full capacity of your lungs. If you do begin to feel breathless because the space is limited by the baby – which can make you feel rather panicky – you will be able to think about breathing into your back, and allow a lengthening in the spine to increase the mobility of the breathing muscles.

Alexander teachers do not teach specific breathing techniques as preparation for labour. Instead they concentrate on teaching you to breathe well. Poor breathing habits are worked upon, giving particular attention to 'breath-holding' and 'gasping' because these are habits that occur most commonly during labour.

Alexander teachers also encourage you to become aware of your breathing as a way of getting in touch with your body and its rhythms. Focusing on your breathing when it is deep and unrestricted is a way of calming the mind, and accessing an inner quietness that will prepare you for the intensity of the emotions you may feel during your labour.

The whispered ah (see pages 76–8) should be practised regularly throughout pregnancy. It is effective in improving your breathing generally and is another way of restoring your emotional equilibrium. It can be used as a tool in labour and birth for keeping the breathing free and rhythmic. Puffy cheek breathing (see page 79) is also useful for releasing tension.

'In my ante-natal classes we had an unhibited Italian who made us get on to all fours and start vocalizing. This helped because you weren't looking at anyone else and feeling embarrassed, and it made it easier to go inside myself. Although we all hated practising in the class, when I went into labour it was one of the most important things I used.' *Jenny*

Vocalizing in Pregnancy

Vocalizing – for example singing or chanting – exercises muscles throughout the body and is thus a very good way of building up strength and stamina. It also develops lung capacity. In fact, any form of vocalization, if performed with good use in mind, can help to improve your use and bring you back into a more balanced state. Making sounds can be used as a way to connect into your inner self, which should help you to tune into the natural rhythms of birth.

For a great many women making sounds makes it much easier to cope with the intensity of contractions when they are in labour. It is a way of tuning in to the pain, and of expressing it, instead of the pain becoming internalized as tension in the body. Vocalizing involves focusing on the sound you make and using it as a way of keeping control. It is important that you do not let it turn into screaming, as screaming is extremely exhausting and can make you feel even more distressed. You are also likely to have a sore throat after the birth, as letting the breath out in an uncontrolled rush damages the vocal chords.

It may sound artificial to suggest that you practise making sounds before the actual labour, but in fact it is important that you do. You need to learn to connect your voice into your body, and you need to train up the correct muscles for producing the voice. If you are using your voice well, the abdominal muscles and the action of your lower ribs will be providing the breath for the sound. If you are using your voice badly, you will be pushing the sound from your upper chest and throat.

An ideal exercise for preparing the voice for labour is the whispered ah. Chanting and singing are also excellent. If you are practising the Alexander Technique with a group of pregnant women you will find that chanting together, or singing rounds, is an enlivening and uplifting experience. The antenatal classes run by the French obstetrician Michel Odent at the clinic in Pithiviers, France, used to be group singing sessions. It is thought that singing and chanting release endorphins (see pages 122–3), the body's natural way of suppressing pain and anxiety.

6 Common Complaints in Pregnancy

There are a number of conditions that are accepted as inevitable in pregnancy; some of these are a direct result of poor posture and use at a time when the ligaments are lax and you are carrying a lot of extra weight, and as such are avoidable. Some complaints, of course, are the result of the baby growing in what is actually a very confined area; other complaints such as heartburn and varicose veins have other causes as well. Because of this, good use cannot always prevent them, but it can do a lot to alleviate them.

Problem areas
The Back

You may experience pain in any part of the back during pregnancy, and this is usually a direct consequence of carrying the extra weight of the baby poorly. Instead of maintaining our upright posture with an even distribution of tension throughout the musculature of the body, we over-contract some muscles and allow some to be too relaxed. The pain is caused by either the over-tensing of the muscles or the excessive strain on the lax muscles and ligaments. Backache during pregnancy is not something women should see as a necessary evil. With improved use these aches and pains can be alleviated.

There are, of course, other causes of backache. For example, prolapse of an intervertebral disc can be caused by an organic disease, or result from an injury. If you are unfortunate enough to suffer from such a condition then it is even more imperative that you use yourself well in pregnancy.

Sacroiliac pain is the classic low-back pain that occurs in pregnancy. It is usually located immediately over these joints, or it can be experienced internally in the pelvis, the pain often being severe, even incapacitating. This can make standing and walking very uncomfortable, and can cause limping. Straining the sacroiliac joints is not only very painful but it can lead to long-term problems with the back.

The sacroiliac area is particularly vulnerable, because the weight of the whole upper body is transmitted into the pelvis, through these joints. In order to be stable enough to support this weight, the sacroiliac joints are held together by strong ligaments that allow very little movement.

In pregnancy, this area becomes even more vulnerable, because of the softening of the ligaments. This allows greater movement, which makes them less stable and more susceptible to strain. The pain is caused by this extra unaccustomed movement of the joint, or sometimes misalignment of the joint, and also by the constant strain on the surrounding ligaments.

It is obvious that having poor use will put additional strain on this already vulnerable area. Slumping – letting the spine collapse – means that the weight of the upper body falls heavily into the sacroiliac area. Excessive hollowing of the lower back also affects the way the weight of the upper body is distributed on to these joints.

With good use, however, the likelihood of having sacroiliac problems is considerably reduced. Directing the spine to lengthen upwards, and inhibiting the desire to pull down and slump, creates a lightness of the upper body. In this way the muscles provide support for the joint rather than putting additional strain on the ligaments, and the weight is distributed on to the joints more evenly.

If you do suffer from pain in the sacroiliac region, take great care with twisting movements of the spine in relationship to the pelvis, such as rolling over in bed or getting into a car, because this opens and closes the joint and increases the pain. Pulling your knees in towards each other also puts a strain on the sacroiliac joints, so remember your Alexander directions to let your knees go forwards and away and keep as free as possible in the hip joints.

Pain felt running down the back of the leg is commonly known as **sciatica**. It follows the pathway of the sciatic nerve – through the buttock, down the back of the leg, behind the knee, sometimes extending to the ankle. Sciatic pain is well known because so many people suffer from it, quite apart from pregnant women. The underlying cause, as well as sacroiliac problems, is often years of faulty use. Especially harmful are habits that involve pressing down into the hips, such as standing with locked knees, or with all the weight on one leg, and sitting slumped or with the legs crossed.

In the long term you are more likely to avoid developing sciatica if you have good use. Immediate relief can be found by assuming a position that shifts the weight of the baby away from the area in which it is causing pressure. Most popular are all fours and rocking. An effective way to release muscular tension in this area is a variation of the semi-supine position: instead of placing the feet on the floor, rest the calves and feet on the seat of a low armchair or sofa and allow the knees to be soft and loose and to turn outwards a little.

The Feet

During pregnancy the **arches** of the feet are extremely vulnerable, owing to a combination of the extra weight being carried and the increased laxity of the ligaments. This can result in the ligaments being permanently overstretched and a consequent flattening or collapse of the architecture of the foot. (Many women notice this has happened when they find that after their pregnancy they need to take a larger size in shoes.)

Fallen arches cause pain, which some women experience only first thing in the morning; others feel discomfort after the birth. It is important to prevent the arches collapsing because damaged arches affect upright posture and movement.

The increased weight and laxity of the ligaments are physiological factors and as such may be unavoidable. However, with good use you can lessen the likelihood of the arches falling if you maintain good use. The common misuse in pregnancy of standing with the weight of the body falling on to the front of the foot puts additional strain on the ligaments and weakens the arches. With good use the weight of the body should fall through the ankle slightly in front of the ankle joint, in which case it will be distributed evenly over the whole of the foot.

Footwear is particularly important during your pregnancy. High heels throw your body weight forward and increase the strain on the front of the foot; you will also tense muscles in the rest of your body in order to maintain your balance. Shoes that are good for your use have low heels and should give adequate support. While you are at home it is good to go without shoes to allow the foot to move unrestrictedly.

It is obviously not wise to be on your feet for long periods. Do take regular rests and put your feet up, either sitting or lying down. Certain types of exercise are beneficial for both the ligaments and muscles of the foot. Swimming is particularly good in pregnancy as your feet are not weight-bearing and are used in a full range of movements.

The Ribs

From about the thirtieth week of pregnancy until the baby drops into the pelvis some women experience pain in the **lower ribcage**. This is caused by the uterus pressing against the lower ribs and the muscles and ligaments. It is more usually felt on the right side because the uterus is slightly rotated to that side. As a result of overall poor use, many people lessen the amount of room available in the ribcage by over-contracting the musculature. In Alexander work we aim to free up this musculature which results in more space and freer movement of the lower ribcage. Slumping forwards also increases the likelihood of the uterus pressing against the ribcage, so keeping your back lengthened and upright will help avoid this.

The Pelvis

The hormonal softening that affects the ligaments in the sacroiliac joints also affects the **symphysis pubis** (the pubic bone), which tends to ease apart slightly towards the end of pregnancy as the baby moves down into the pelvis. This may make the area feel tender, and movements that stress the joint, such as moving from one leg to the other, may cause pain. The instructions we give you for standing and walking (see pages 67–70) will help you to avoid this.

Women often experience aching or a feeling of heaviness in the pelvis, particularly towards the end of pregnancy as the baby drops lower. Irritation of the pelvic nerves, caused by either the pressure of the baby's head or excessive muscular tension, causes sharp but intermittent pains in the groin, and down the legs, as well as a niggling, general achiness.

You may also experience pain in the **round ligaments**, which are the ligaments on either side of the uterus which anchor it to the pubic bone. As the uterus grows, it stretches these ligaments upwards and they become susceptible to spasm, which can be felt as a 'stitch' or pain in the groin, quite common during pregnancy. If you take care not to move in a quick and jerky way and instead think of moving your head, neck and back in one piece, you can avoid pulling on these ligaments.

Other problems

Heartburn

In the last three or four months of pregnancy many women suffer from heartburn as the sphincter muscle at the top of the stomach becomes more relaxed. This allows the acid contents of the stomach back up into the throat, causing a burning sensation. The uterus pushing against the stomach encourages this regurgitation.

Your use is particularly important at this time when your organs have become so cramped. Slumping forwards leaves even less room for the stomach. The more upright you can keep your spine, and the freer your musculature, the less likely you are to suffer from the complaint. Eating smaller and more frequent meals is one effective way to avoid heartburn. It is also important to avoid movements or positions that push the uterus against the stomach, or bending forwards with a rounded back – which is easy to do if you already have small children.

If you have indigestion or heartburn (or you have just indulged in a large meal!) the best remedy is to find a position where the pressure of the uterus against your stomach is reduced. In the daytime use a chair that encourages you to sit upright, and think about giving your directions. At night use three or four pillows to prop yourself up. You can also try going on to your hands and knees in the crawling position. This allows the uterus to drop away from the stomach, and gives you a little bit of extra space for your abdominal organs.

'One thing I found a real relief if I had heartburn was crawling. Being on all fours, I had that extra help from gravity, with the bump hanging, taking the pressure off my stomach. It made such a difference. I used to do it after an evening meal – it was such a relief.' *Monique*

Varicose Veins

During pregnancy there is an increased possibility of varicose veins developing or worsening. They most commonly occur in the legs and in the anal canal (haemorrhoids), and less frequently in the vulva. Because of hormonal softening which relaxes the vein walls, an increase in blood circulating in the body, and the pressure from the enlarging uterus obstructing the veins in the pelvic region, it becomes more difficult for the blood from the pelvic region and the legs to return to the heart. The pressure in the veins can build up and cause the blood to pool; this then damages the veins, which become varicose. In addition to it being a painful condition, varicose veins are unsightly. They are not easy to get rid of, so it is worth doing all you can to avoid letting them develop in the first place.

As well as the potential causes in pregnancy mentioned above, there is also a hereditary predisposition to developing them. You cannot alter any of these, but the way you use yourself has a great deal to do with whether varicose veins develop or not. If you have poor use and you have allowed your spine to collapse you will be increasing the already considerable downward pressure of the weight of the baby on to your pelvis and legs. In addition, you will be tightening the muscles of the pelvis and the legs excessively to try to stabilize your posture, causing the circulation in the lower body to be restricted. As your balance improves with Alexander lessons and the weight of the baby becomes supported by the back muscles, the downward pressure will ease, the circulation will improve, and varicose veins will be less likely to occur.

To help prevent varicose veins in the legs, avoid positions that encourage the blood to pool in the legs. Sitting with one leg crossed over the other is a very difficult habit to break, but it does restrict circulation in the legs considerably. Not wanting varicose veins is a good incentive to stop. Standing still for long periods also makes it difficult for the blood to return to the heart. If you have to sit or stand still for long periods exercises such as ankle rotating (if sitting), or gentle walking on the spot without lifting your toes off the ground (if standing) works the muscles which helps pump the blood back to the heart. Wearing support stockings will also help alleviate the discomfort and prevent the condition becoming worse.

To avoid vulval and anal varicosities, try not to become constipated, and do not strain when defecating. This puts additional pressure on the pelvic area, so make sure you have a good diet with plenty of roughage and fluids, and instead of straining try releasing your pelvic floor, allowing it to bulge downwards, and give short pushes with the abdominal muscles, as you exhale. (Never hold your breath.) Stimulating the blood flow by practising pelvic floor contractions regularly helps relieve the congestion in this area.

Oedema

The body retains more fluid in pregnancy, so some oedema – water retention which causes swelling – is quite normal. Always get proper medical advice on any oedema, because it can also be a symptom of several more serious conditions. It is most common in the feet and ankles, usually occurring in the last twelve weeks of pregnancy. The oedema disappears with rest and usually will not be present after a night's sleep. Avoiding being on your feet for long periods, resting with your legs elevated and gentle leg exercises are beneficial.

Some swelling in the hands and fingers can also occur, causing stiffness in the fingers and often a tingling sensation. The swelling can also cause carpel tunnel syndrome, a fairly common condition of pregnancy in which there is a shooting pain and numbness in the wrists and hands, especially the long finger, index finger and thumb. The symptoms usually disappear directly after the delivery, sometimes literally within minutes, although some numbness in the hands may last a little longer.

The cause of this oedema is unknown, but again the Technique can bring some welcome relief to the discomfort. Slumping, or pulling down in front, rounds the shoulders and restricts circulation. Releasing up the front and thinking of widening across the chest, and an image of 'space in the armpits' will help. When sitting in an armchair or at a table you can rest your elbows and point your fingers up, directing the forearm to lengthen. Orthopaedic supports to hold the wrist still (which helps) and the hand in a resting position can be obtained from your obstetric physiotherapist. You should also avoid tight bra straps pulling on your shoulders,.

PART THREE
Labour and Birth

There is much talk about choice in childbirth. Usually this means having the right to choose between a home birth or hospital, whether one is allowed to move around or not, whether or not to use analgesia, or how the delivery is conducted. It is crucial that women should be able to make these very important choices about such a major event in their lives. However, in the Alexander Technique, the concept of choice is on a more fundamental level, and lies at the heart of the Technique.

The Alexander Technique gives women a real and practical choice concerning the course and outcome of their labour. Although labour is a very demanding situation in which to practise your Alexander skills, the choice you have is how you use yourself and how you respond. Rather than becoming anxious and tense, you can choose to respond to the challenge of labour by inhibiting this response. Thus you can keep your muscles free from unnecessary tension, allow the breathing to continue freely, and let all your energy be directed towards the process of giving birth to your baby.

'The Alexander work I had done made it possible for me to let myself go. I sang a lot to myself between contractions. Alexander inhibition helped me to control my body with my mind. It gave me time to stop the automatic reaction to tense up and have the ability to completely relax in the area where the pain was – across my lower abdomen and legs.' *Margaret*

'My sense at the time was that my uterus was doing exactly what it needed to do to expel the baby and that my body was the vehicle it was using – all I had to do was keep my body in a position that would most facilitate this and make sure I wasn't wasting my energy by tensing up the rest of my body'. *Jacqueline*

---

7 Use in Labour

'My technique is based on inhibition, the inhibition of undesirable, unwanted responses to stimuli, and hence it is primarily a technique for the development of the control of human reaction.' *F.M. Alexander*

Birth is a total experience, involving your whole self, and the recognition of the implicit unity of mind and body (or psycho-physical unity), which is central to the Alexander Technique, is vital to our understanding of how we can use the Technique in labour and birth.

A common understanding of natural birth is that all we have to do is let go of 'control' and our instinctive nature will take over; that if we simply trust our bodies then all will be well. However, the problem with this is that, unlike animals, we do not operate purely instinctively but have a conscious mind that affects our behaviour. Alexander saw that in order to improve our functioning we have to bring our behaviour into the conscious realm, and he called this 'constructive conscious control'.

Conscious control in the Alexander sense, as we have already seen (see page 23), does not mean a superimposed or forced control, but instead a kind of conscious 'guidance' of our use, which allows the natural process to continue without interference.

We believe that women need to use this 'conscious control' of themselves in labour, otherwise the natural processes of childbirth can be hindered by excessive muscular tightening in response to the pain of labour, in the same way as the body's mechanisms for balance and movement are hindered. By having conscious control we are able to let our 'instinctive' nature function. , instinctive here referring to the body's innate mechanisms.

'When an investigation comes to be made, it will be found that every single thing we are doing in the work is exactly what is being done in Nature where the conditions are right, the difference being that we are learning to do it consciously.' *F.M.Alexander*

Maintaining Good Use in Labour

There are different ways in which you can maintain this 'conscious control' during labour. If you have been practising the Alexander Technique in your daily lives for some time, it will have become second nature to inhibit and direct. You can consciously use this as a tool in labour. So, at the start of each contraction, inhibit and direct, that is, pause and 'listen' to what is going on, and then, while thinking of inhibiting any unnecessary muscular tension, think, *'Let the neck be free, to allow the head to go forward and up, and the back to lengthen and widen, and allow the knees to go forward and away.'* In practice it is often more beneficial to simply think '*neck free*' and you will find that if you keep your neck muscles released the musculature of the whole of the body is freer. In between contractions, once again 'listen' to your body to see if there is any excessive tension left over from the contraction, and inhibit and direct to help you come back to a balanced and relaxed state.

Consciously using inhibition and direction is incredibly effective during labour, but for many women it is difficult to do this in such an intense situation, and in fact it can act as a distraction. As an alternative we have given you some rather more tangible tools that you can use directly in labour. These are the different procedures – monkey, squatting, lunging, kneeling, all fours, whispered ah, puffy cheek breathing – and vocalizing, which all encourage good use and help you to keep muscular tension to the minimum required.

As well as using these various tools, it is important that you have an understanding of the Technique in your body. Many actors study the Alexander Technique, for it greatly improves their performance. However, they will tell you that when they are on stage they are concentrating on their performance – they are not consciously thinking 'neck free', and so on. They have the skills and they can trust them and allow them to enhance their performance. In the same way when you are giving birth, having good use means that you are already using inhibition and direction. It may not be what you are thinking about consciously, but it will be apparent in the way you use yourself and the way you respond to the changing situation. You learn the skills beforehand and they become part of you. All the benefits of good use are there for you.

'I have found that in this process of acquiring a conscious direction of use my pupils gradually develop a higher standard of sensory awareness or appreciation of what they are doing in the use of themselves, so that when it comes to carrying out a course of activity they have decided upon, they possess a criterion within themselves which will enable them to judge whether the use they are employing is right or not for the purpose.' *F.M. Alexander*

Means Whereby in Labour

' . . . where the means whereby are right for the purpose, desired ends will come. They are inevitable. Why then be concerned as to the manner and speed of their coming? We should reserve all thought, energy and concern for the means whereby we may commend the manner of their coming.' *F.M. Alexander*

'We often want to know in advance what something will feel like, how much it will hurt, or how long it will take. Going into labour and giving birth is an obvious situation where we cannot know in advance what it will be like. The means-whereby approach helps us stay in the present and deal with the unpredictable.' *Brita*

When Alexander talks about 'means whereby' he means the reasoned steps towards achieving a desired goal. This philosophy is useful in childbirth, where our goal is given – to deliver the baby! In labour it means taking events as they occur, one by one, keeping as free from unnecessary tension as possible, and not worrying about what is to come.

Sometimes in the middle of labour women feel as if it is going to go on for ever and wish that they could just walk away from it. If you start to think like this, it is very easy to feel overwhelmed by the whole experience and begin to panic. If you can keep an attitude of 'listening' to the sensations of the contractions and how your body responds, inhibiting and directing if possible, it will help you to stay in the present and make it much easier for you to cope. In the rests between contractions, so long as you are not worrying about the next contraction starting, you can go into such a deep state of relaxation that a minute feels like half an hour's deep sleep.

However, even though you are staying in the present and taking each event as it comes, you should not lose sight of what your contractions are achieving – the birth of your baby.

'As time passed the contractions became more painful and lasted longer. There was also less time in between them. This was a critical period for me. I had no idea how long it would be before Jake would be born – would it be two hours away or twenty-four hours? How would I last? The key was thinking Direction, just letting each contraction happen, and then when it passed I let go of the tension. This worked remarkably well. And as I was so successful in being able to direct in between contractions I felt tremendous relief. I actually was able to rest and restore my energies in those one or two minute breaks. My confidence was really shored up by this and Richard and I soon found ourselves joking around and laughing. I have a vague memory of saying how normal things seemed between those contractions – not like I was in the middle of the most intense experience of my life. I found it helped to face the contractions one at a time and to remember that each contraction was bringing me nearer to my baby.' *Debbie*

Visualization

If you do not know what happens in childbirth, you may feel fearful. Many women, to express it rather crudely, look at the size of the 'bump', think of the size of their vagina, and panic. Throughout the book we have included explanations and pictures of the anatomy and physiology of labour and birth so that you understand the mechanics, and what you are likely to experience.

This knowledge of the birthing process can be used whilst you are in labour as a way of 'thinking' into your body. During the first stage, with each contraction you may like to picture the muscle fibres of the uterus 'pulling up' to open up the cervix around your baby's head. In the second stage you may like to picture each contraction pushing your baby on her journey through the birth canal, and of your pelvic floor releasing and opening up to let her through. Not everyone finds it easy to 'think' in pictures, however, so an alternative is to 'think' in words. For example, at each contraction you may be telling your cervix to open, or you may be telling your pelvic floor to release as you push down in the second stage. This is not a way to distract you or remove you from what is going on in your body, but rather a way of focusing your attention and tuning into your body. It is a way of staying in the present, and with what is going on.

Thinking into your body specifically about what you would like to happen in the course of labour is similar to giving yourself Alexander directions. The effect of directing the labour this way has not been scientifically investigated, but we would hypothesize that it has a positive influence on the birthing process.

Relaxation in Activity

Although practising the Alexander Technique has a very calming and relaxing effect, it is not like the kinds of relaxation techniques that encourage people to go into a passive state. What you learn from the Alexander Technique could better be called 'relaxation in activity'.

By 'relaxing in activity', you will be able to stay attentive and respond when necessary to whatever is happening around you. By maintaining overall integrity and co-ordination, the general levels of tension within the body will be lowered, ensuring that breathing remains unrestricted (and thus able to respond to your body's need for oxygen) and allowing greater freedom of movement to adopt helpful positions. You will be skilled at noticing and letting go of any tightening and resistance in response to the contractions, so that you have minimal muscular activity in the parts of the body that are not being used, and the involuntary processes of labour are able to function.

The major advantage of staying relaxed is that you will not get so tired; it is tiredness that intensifies your perception of the pain, and often pure exhaustion marks the start of problems in labour. If you can stay as relaxed as possible as labour progresses, all your energy can focus into the uterus so it can do its job in the most efficient way. With more energy available you will be able to keep the muscles of the birth canal and pelvic floor relaxed so that they do not resist the expulsive work of the uterus. And when you finally push your baby out you will be awake and alert to appreciate the moment of birth, and those first precious moments together.

Being upright with the back inclined slightly forwards is the most advantageous position for childbirth – for both the mother and the baby.

'Active' Labour: the Advantages

With increasing medical intervention, starting with the use of forceps and more recently analgesia, continuous foetal monitoring and induction, it has become necessary for women to assume a recumbent position for the convenience of the medical attendants who administer these procedures. For the purpose of childbirth, though, lying down is probably one of the most disadvantageous positions that can be adopted.

Throughout history and worldwide, where medical intervention does not dictate a position, women instinctively assume a variety of upright and crouching positions. The most common are standing (with the upper body inclined

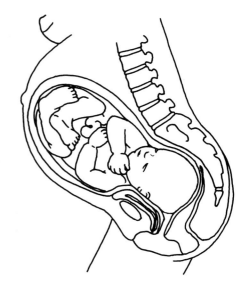

forwards), kneeling, squatting, and all fours, and these are the most physiologically advantageous positions for childbirth. Interestingly, from an Alexander perspective, these positions are also best because they encourage good use and the best overall functioning of the whole body.

An upright position, particularly with the spine inclined forwards, assists the physical mechanics that apply during labour in a number of ways:

- The mother is working with the forces of gravity; the baby's head is brought into direct contact with the cervix, which stimulates contractions, and the weight of the baby creates a downward pressure in the pelvis.
- Because the inlet to the pelvis slopes forwards very slightly, the baby enters the pelvis at an angle that helps her descend more easily, and helps her head flex (tucking the chin on to the chest), thus reducing the diameter that has to enter the pelvis.
- During contractions the uterus tilts away from the spine, and forwards on to the abdominal wall. An upright position assists this forwards tilt and consequently the uterus can contract more efficiently.
- The joints in the pelvis – the sacroiliac and the symphysis pubis – are free to ease apart to allow more room for the baby's head to descend through the pelvis. In a squatting position the overall size of the pelvis is increased by as much as 30 per cent.
- The pelvic floor is at its most relaxed, and the pressure of the baby's head is directed on to the perineum, a wedge of muscles that is designed to thin out and allow the delivery of the baby (see page 115).
- When the mother is lying flat on her back, the weight of the uterus falls directly on the major blood vessels that return blood to the heart. This produces a fall in blood pressure in the mother, and a reduced supply of oxygenated blood going to the baby. If the mother is upright, her circulation is improved and the baby receives a better supply of oxygen.

In addition to physical factors, the positions that you adopt during labour make a huge difference to how you feel psychologically. Studies have shown that when lying down many women feel vulnerable and that everything is being done to them, irrespective of their wishes. 'I felt like a beached whale,' is a frequent comment. In direct contrast, women overwhelmingly prefer to be free to move around in the first stage and to find for themselves the most comfortable position for delivery. Upright postures make women feel in control of the situation, and this increases their ability to cope. They feel more involved and can participate more easily.

If you are aware of the effect of different positions on uterine activity, you can change the tempo of the contractions. This again gives you some control over the labour and a feeling of being in charge. If you wish to speed up labour you can use upright postures, squatting, and any movement generally. If it is going too fast you can use reclining positions, or adopt an all fours position with your head resting on your forearms and your bottom in the air.

In an active labour, a high level of endorphins (our bodies' natural painkillers) are released to produce a natural analgesia. Endorphin production is known to be stimulated by sustained movement. There are also studies that have demonstrated that when people feel that they are in control endorphins are secreted, and that when they feel out of control, they secrete adrenalin-type hormones that prevent endorphin production.

If a woman feels confident in herself, she will tune into her body and instinctively find positions that help the labour. She will adopt these positions not because she is thinking consciously about the mechanics of labour but because it feels the most comfortable way to cope with the contractions. For example, in a labour where the baby is lying with his back against the mother's spine – a 'posterior presentation' – the woman will often spontaneously adopt an all fours position. This relieves the backache caused by the baby pressing on her sacral nerves. Interestingly this is also the best position for getting the baby to rotate in the pelvis into an 'anterior presentation', which is a better position for the birth.

A striking characteristic of labour is the fact that women, if they are free to do so, will change position frequently, and spontaneously rock and sway and 'belly dance'. As Alexander teachers we recommend and encourage movement in labour. If you stay in one position any tension in response to the pain of the contraction becomes locked into the musculature – and increases your perception of the pain. A tangible way to make the labour less painful is to translate this excessive muscular tension into continual gentle and flowing movements, based on these Alexander procedures. Movement also heightens our sensory awareness, so it is also a way to stay more in touch with our bodies.

Overall, studies into the advantages of moving freely in labour and being upright for the delivery have shown that:

- Labour time is reduced – both first and second stage
- Less pain is experienced, therefore less pain relief is needed
- The speeding up of labour with the hormone oxytocin is less likely to be necessary
- Fewer episiotomies are needed
- Fewer forceps deliveries are performed
- Women feel more involved in their labour

For the baby:

- Foetal heart rate during labour is less likely to be affected
- The condition of the baby is better at birth
- There will be less direct pressure on the baby's neck, thereby protecting the delicate mechanisms of head control, which play an important role in the baby's motor development. In the short term, disturbance of these mechanisms can cause breastfeeding difficulties where the baby can't latch on or suckle properly, or perhaps can only feed from one side.

Finally, a word to recommend that you rest as much as you can. Although birth positions help labour immensely, you do not need to be active all the time. Conserve your energy, and use your rest periods to take the time to adjust to what is happening, to the sensations and your emotional responses. There are resting positions (see pages 71–3) which maintain good use of the body, and many of them give you the physiological advantages of upright positions as well.

Positions for Labour

Monkey in Labour

Monkey is vital in labour. The forward inclination of the back assists the uterus to contract more efficiently and helps you to maintain good use. It is helpful to have something to support your weight, such as bookshelves, banisters or walls. (In traditional societies a birthing pole or a rope was often used for hanging from during childbirth.) Many women find that being supported by another person is particularly helpful, because it also gives them much needed emotional support. Some women like to give birth in this more upright, hanging position, while being supported either by one person behind, or a person on either side.

The monkey is also the best position for a birth supporter to adopt when supporting the woman, as it requires the least amount of muscular effort to maintain, thus minimizing fatigue. The supporter also maximizes flexibility and mobility through his or her body, which is important when supporting a labouring woman – unlike holding a heavy object which is static, the woman will be moving in response to her contractions.

Circling and rocking movements are used spontaneously by women in labour. When in a shallow monkey, you have much more freedom in the hip joints, and you can circle your pelvis, or rock from side to side in 'belly dancing' movements. If you have practised t'ai chi you will know rocking from side to side as a warm-up exercise. Having your partner's hands on your pelvis, guiding the movement, helps you to keep your attention centred in your pelvis. This makes it easier to keep your pelvic floor, as well as your upper body, free of tension.

Hanging in monkey supported from behind

With your partner in monkey, supporting you with his hands under your armpits (*below left*), you can 'hang' either in a very shallow monkey or slightly deeper. He may like to lean with his back against a wall to make it less tiring for him.

Facing partner

For this very comforting position (*below right*) simply lean into your partner in a shallow monkey; you can circle or rock together.

Leaning against wall
This is a good way (*left*) to take support and get a little rest, while at the same time remaining mobile and active during labour.

Leaning back against partner
Another 'dancing' movement (*below left*). If you let yourselves lean into each other fully, there should be no effort on either part.

Hanging from (or leaning on) rail
A secure rail or banister gives strong support (*below right*) and yet allows great mobility during active labour.

Lunge in Labour

A lunging movement releases the inner thigh and pelvic floor muscles wonderfully. During contractions try shifting the weight backwards and forwards between the front and the back leg. You can do this either with both feet on the ground, or an alternative that women find helpful is to have one foot on a low stool. For both of these you may like to place a hand on a table or chair for support.

Shifting weight backwards and forwards
Having your partner gently guide your lunging (*above left*) helps to focus your attention on the movement.

One foot up on a chair or step
A great way of being active in early labour (*above right*). Rocking or shifting the weight forwards and backwards can help ease the pain of contractions and relax the pelvic floor.

Leaning against fireplace or shelf
You can take support from a piece of furniture or a fixture (make sure it is secure) during contractions, and then walk and move about freely between contractions (*above left*).

Facing partner
A good way to be close to and supported by your partner during contractions and while resting in between (*above right*).

Squatting in Labour

Squatting is the most physiologically advantageous position for birth. It creates pressure in the pelvis, and brings the baby's head strongly against the cervix, which makes the contractions stronger. It also increases the amount of room in the pelvis and facilitates the descent of the baby.

Remember that squatting is very tiring; it is not really necessary to spend a lot of time in a deep squat in the first stage of labour, and it is important that you don't tire yourself out unnecessarily. Other upright positions are just as beneficial. Squatting is more useful and appropriate in the second stage of labour. However, as mentioned above, if the baby is not yet engaged, squatting with each contraction and then walking between contractions is a very good way to stimulate contractions to come more frequently and help with the descent of the baby.

'Hanging squat' on bed, supported by partner in front
It is easier for your partner to support you in a hanging squat (*right*) when you are on the bed instead of on the floor, as he does not have to bend so low.

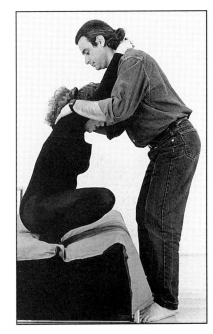

Supported by partner sitting on chair or bed
You can squat either facing your partner or with your back to him, arms over his legs (*below left and right*). These are very comfortable for both you and your supporter. They are particularly good if the partner has a back problem.

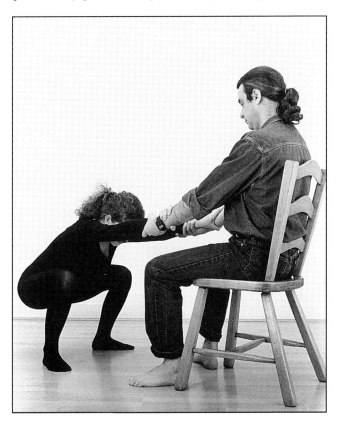

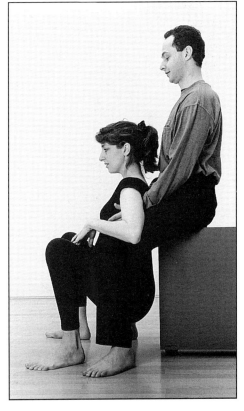

Squatting on bed, supported by partner behind
Again, in this position (*left*) the partner can take a fairly active role without too much effort.

Squat on bed, supported both sides
The extra comfort of two supporters (*right*) makes it easier for you to relax. They can either put their arms under your armpits or you can put your arms around their necks, with their arms around your back. You can either hang in this position or if your supporters are in a deep monkey or are kneeling they can have one knee each under your bottom.

Kneeling in Labour

Kneeling offers many of the advantages of monkey and squatting, but it has the added bonus that it is much less tiring. In fact, kneeling is an excellent way of resting between contractions at any stage of labour; either have your bottom on your heels, or, for a more active position, kneel up. If you do sit on your heels, however comfortable it feels, do not stay in the same position for too long as the legs can go numb. You need to be supported as much as possible, so lean on a bed or chair, a pile of cushions or on your partner.

Kneeling is also a popular birth position. Again, you will need support from something that you can safely lean against, like a bed or a person, and you will, of course, be kneeling up. Half kneeling and half squatting is also a possibility for giving birth, but once again you need support.

Half kneeling and half squatting leaning on chair (or partner's knees)
A more active position (*above*), in both first and second stage, good for stretching the pelvic floor and allowing mobility in the hip joints. Try rocking backwards and forwards between the knee and the foot.

Kneeling facing partner on chair, holding on to his arms
Gives a secure support from your partner against the powerful forces of the bearing down contractions (*below*).

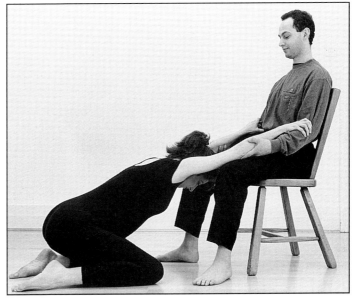

Upright kneeling supported by partner
This is similar to a hanging squat or monkey (*left*), but you are less likely to tighten the thigh muscles and it is not so tiring for your legs. Your partner should be in monkey.

Hanging from bar and kneeling
Another quite active position (*right*) where you are very much in control.

All Fours in Labour

Women in many different cultures spontaneously give birth on all fours. In an all fours position, with the trunk horizontal, gravity is not directing the weight of the baby's head strongly on to the cervix, and therefore the contractions are not being stimulated so directly. Hence if the labour is going too fast, and the woman feels overwhelmed, she can use this position to slow down the pace a little. In the second stage this is particularly useful to control the rate of delivery, giving the pelvic floor muscles time to stretch and avoid unnecessary tearing.

All fours is the position a woman should use when the baby is lying with its back against the mother's spine (a posterior presentation). It is commonly called 'a backache labour', because the baby's head is pressing

'By this time I was on the delivery table and I tried squatting supported by my husband. But the pressure of the baby's head on my pelvic floor felt so great at that point that I felt extremely uncomfortable – as if I'd burst. So I turned over on to all fours which was an immediate improvement and I felt really good. I had no desire to lie or half sit at all.' *Penelope Bowund*, 'Birth On All Fours', A.R.M. No. 10, June 1981

on the sacral nerves in the lower back. When the baby is lying in this position it takes longer for him to descend into the pelvis, so the labour can be quite protracted. With the mother on her hands and knees, the pressure of the baby is taken off the sacral nerves, thus relieving the backache. This position also helps the baby to rotate into an anterior presentation and descend into the pelvis.

The all fours position also allows the pelvis to open up to its greatest capacity and promotes relaxation of the pelvic floor. It is therefore very useful where the baby is large, and, in the rare cases when the baby's shoulders get stuck during delivery (shoulder dystocia), this is the position the midwife would ask you to adopt to get the baby out safely.

'When the midwife said I should push with the next contraction I gave a gentle spontaneous push without holding my breath. Then I was surprised to hear her telling me to pant, and lifting up my maternity dress so that I could see between my legs I saw the baby's head being born! About half a minute later the next contraction came. I pushed gently again and the baby's body slid out. There he was! This time I didn't tear or graze either.' *Penelope Bowund*, 'Birth On All Fours', A.R.M. No. 10, June 1981

Breathing in Labour

Your body needs different amounts of oxygen in different circumstances and will automatically adjust your breathing to meet these demands. In labour our approach is that you should let your breathing respond spontaneously to the need for oxygen for both you and the baby, and with the changing intensity of the contractions. Labour is indeed hard work, in all likelihood harder than any other activity you perform in your life, so it is essential that you can breathe freely and unrestrictedly to be able to supply the huge amount of oxygen that you need. If you can maintain your good use in labour, then the breathing apparatus will be able to work to fulfil these needs.

If you respond to the pain and anxiety of labour by tightening your muscles (particularly the neck), you will find that your breathing will become restricted. You may go into poor breathing patterns, the most frequently occurring of these being hyperventilation. This is caused by holding the breath, which makes the ribcage tense and restricts the movement of the diaphragm; you then begin to feel short of breath and start gasping for air, which in turn allows too much oxygen in your blood stream and makes you feel dizzy and tingly.

By a happy coincidence, the positions that we suggest you use – the monkey, the squat and the lunge – are the most advantageous positions for releasing the tension that interferes with breathing and stimulating full and deep breathing. In fact Alexander asked his students to do monkey as a way to teach them to breathe more fully.

If you are maintaining this deep, free and rhythmical breathing, you will be able to use the awareness of the breath as a way to get in tune with your body. You can let the rhythm of the breath be dictated by the strength of the contractions and you can use your breath as a way to let yourself surrender to the powerful forces of labour. This is very different from the breathing techniques where you keep 'control' of the situation by using your breathing as something to focus your attention on as a way to distract yourself, or distance yourself, from the contractions and other sensations in your body.

Vocalizing in Labour

When you are in labour, as soon as you feel the urge to vocalize, let the sound arise in a quiet way, instead of holding it back for as long as possible because you think you should not make a noise, and in your own good time start making sounds, finding your voice inside your body. Gradually let the sound build up in volume. Remember that it should come from deep inside and low down and not be forced through the throat. The kind of sounds that you hear in karate and other martial arts that come straight from the belly are examples of powerful, directed sounds. Movement is very helpful while you are making sounds – it helps to free up the voice. If you are on all fours, lunging or in monkey you can rock gently with the sound.

'When I went into labour the sound built up until I really was bellowing. I couldn't have got through the pain without it. It was like vocalizing the pain out, and was one of the most important things that I used in labour. I spent the whole labour on all fours and I gave birth on all fours, but the vocalizing, throughout the contractions, just got me through. That sound was a focus that helped me keep control of the whole physical thing.' *Jenny*

'When I was pushing the baby out I was shouting and shouting and I knew that I was pulling my head back and would get a sore throat. But at that point I didn't care! I lost my voice for about the next two days.' *Charlotte*

---

8 The Process of Labour

Introduction

A confident approach to labour is achieved not only through the body but also through the mind. Space permits only a brief explanation of labour and birth here, but we encourage you to find out as much as possible. There are now many excellent resources available – books, videos, antenatal classes, etc. Women's bodies are superbly well designed for childbirth, and when the processes of birth are understood, it will be hard for you *not* to have confidence in your ability to give birth.

In the last two or three weeks of a first pregnancy, the baby's head will engage in the pelvis. This means that the head moves down through the inlet of the pelvis. It is said to have engaged when the widest part of the head has passed through the pelvic inlet or brim. (In subsequent babies the head may not engage until labour actually starts.) You will know that this has happened because the whole uterus descends, and usually you will feel more comfortable because there is more room for the internal organs and the diaphragm. Breathing becomes less restricted, and heartburn is relieved.

The onset of labour is not as clear cut as most medical textbooks suggest. In the last few weeks of pregnancy, there will be strong regular contractions, known as Braxton Hicks, which will start and then stop. This is known as 'false labour', but in some cases this is inaccurate because what they are doing is making the cervix efface (i.e. soften and thin out). The cervix before effacement is about 2cm long, and feels quite hard. Once softened and thinned out it is paper thin. When the cervix has thinned out a little, it is possible to feel the baby's head through it.

Women often get a surge of energy a day or so before labour actually begins. You might find yourself busily wanting to sort out cupboards or rearrange things around the house, even feeling wide awake in the night. This can be a sign that you will soon go into labour, but you should try not to tire yourself out; instead try to slow down and rest if this happens (see pages 71–3).

First Stage

What is called the first stage of labour is the time from the onset of true labour until the cervix is fully dilated, which is when it has opened up to 10cm.

One of the possible signs that labour has started is that you have a 'show'. This is when the mucus plug that has sealed off the cervix during pregnancy comes away. It is like a small plug of clear jelly, sometimes slightly blood-stained. If you see it you will easily know what it is. However, it is easy to miss. True labour may still not start for a day or two after the show, but if it is blood tinged that is a sign that there is some contracting and dilating happening in the cervix.

A very clear sign that your baby is on the way is that the membranes surrounding the baby break. The 'waters' or amniotic fluid either gush out or leak more slowly. This can happen before the labour has started, in which case you will probably go into established labour within the next 24 hours. You need to inform your midwife or hospital when your waters break. The waters may break at any time during the first or second stage, and frequently it happens shortly before the start of the second stage. Sometimes they rupture only when the baby's head is being born; membrane on the baby's head, called a 'caul cap', is meant to be a sign of good luck for the baby. Many women experience backache or period-like pains in their lower abdomen as the contractions begin.

A 'textbook' labour is usually described as one that starts with contractions that are weak initially, come every 20 or 30 minutes, and last about 20–30 seconds. These get progressively stronger, more frequent and longer until at the end of the first stage of labour they will be very strong, last 60–90 seconds and come with as little as half a minute between them.

With each contraction the muscle fibres of the uterus progressively shorten and thicken, because they do not return to their original length when they relax between contractions. The cervix is gradually pulled up into the body of the uterus, causing the opening to increase in circumference. This is called dilation. In reality the strength, length and frequency of contractions vary enormously from woman to woman. Dilation becomes progressively faster so that the last 5cm are usually faster than the first five. By the end of the first stage, the cervix will be fully dilated. If the mother is relaxed, there is a harmony between the muscular activity of the upper and lower uterus. The upper segment contracts strongly, while the lower is more passive and allows the stretching and dilating to occur. When this balance is interfered with, the progress of labour is slower.

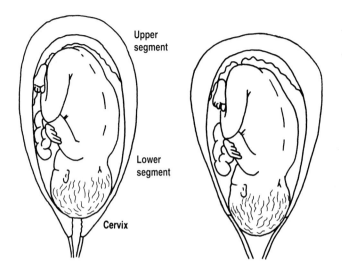

Upper
segment

Lower
segment

Cervix

The cervix dilating could be likened to the neck of a balloon shortening as the balloon is blown up. Once the cervix is fully dilated, the uterus is continuous with the birth canal, and it is time to push the baby out.

Positions for First Stage of Labour

Using the Alexander procedures you have learned, changing your position and moving around as your instinct tells you, will enable you to keep your good use even as the first stage of labour progresses and intensifies.

In early first stage you will probably find the more upright positions best, inclining your back forwards as you have a contraction. As labour progresses you are likely to find the more 'crouching' positions helpful. Walking about, monkey, lunging, kneeling, using your partner for support if necessary, all increase the strength and effectiveness of the contractions. If the baby is not yet engaged, or if you need to speed up contractions, squatting is the position to adopt. Rocking or circling your pelvis, which is something that most women do instinctively, are movements that really do ease the pain of the contractions. You can do this in any position that feels appropriate. Your partner or the midwife needs to make sure that you don't get stuck in an ineffective position because that is a waste of your energy. They can best help by giving you encouragement and suggesting new positions.

Although birth positions help labour immensely, you don't need to be active all the time. Active labour is tiring and you need time to rest. You also need time to adjust to what is happening, to the sensations and your emotional responses, and to centre and calm yourself. If you find that you are resisting letting go to the labour, sometimes this quiet time can be more effective than being active. There are resting positions that maintain good use of the body, and many of these give you the physiological advantages of upright positions as well.

Breathing in First Stage of Labour

The whispered ah is one of the most effective ways to release any muscular tension that is interfering with the breathing mechanism and to restore full and uninterrupted breathing. This breathing exercise could have been tailor-made to help you cope with your labour. We suggest that you greet the beginning of each contraction by breathing out with a whispered ah, keeping your jaw and mouth as soft as possible. You can then allow your breathing to adjust spontaneously to the intensity of the contraction.

In the earlier stages of labour you will probably be able to continue breathing deeply and slowly throughout the contraction, but as the contractions become stronger and more intense, your breathing will automatically change, becoming lighter and moving higher up in the chest. As the contraction recedes you can then go into another whispered ah as a way of releasing any muscular tension that may have built up in response to the contraction. In this way you can let go of the previous contraction, both physically and emotionally. As you rest between the contractions you should return to calm and regular breathing.

The following extract from the account of the birth of their son by Debbie Jay and Richard Levine, who are both Alexander teachers, shows how the whispered ah is an invaluable aid for coping with contractions during labour.

'I was moaning and groaning, "Oh, oh, oh . . ." with my face all scrunched up and my throat badly constricted. Then Richard came up with a brilliant idea. He started coaching me to do the whispered ah! 'Think a smile,' he added. Although this might seem absurd because I felt I had absolutely nothing to smile about, the change in my facial muscles and easing in my throat once I started to do the whispered ah was so profound that I experienced immediate relief! . . . I will always be grateful to Richard, who in staying with the means whereby was inspired to coach me to do this ingenious activity developed by F.M. Alexander. I am convinced that the relief I experienced while doing the whispered ah made it possible for me to go through childbirth without even thinking of asking for pain medication!'

Transition

When you are between 8 and 10cm dilated you enter the stage of labour called transition, which is the turning point or change over from the first to the second stage. For some women the transition is very short and they move easily from one stage to the next, but for others transition can last an hour or more and it can be the most intense and difficult part of labour.

During transition there are many conflicting physical sensations going on in your body all at the same time. The first stage contractions are at their strongest, come very close together, and may have more than one peak of intensity in each contraction. In addition to these contractions you will now have the beginning of the sensations of second stage contractions – and the two together can be overwhelming. You may start shaking, you may go hot, then cold, then hot again in different parts of your body. You may feel sick and you may even vomit. You will probably begin to feel a pressure against your anus, which will feel as though you want to open your bowels. You may also be getting the urge to push.

These conflicting physical feelings are reflected in the conflicting emotions you may feel at this stage. Emotionally it can be the hardest part of childbirth. You may feel frightened, feel that you will not be able to go through with it and that it will never end. You may be irritable and sometimes extremely angry with your partner or the midwife, or you may just want to be left alone. It may all appear like a dream from which you can just walk away. It is not unusual for a woman to announce that she is going home! Your moods may swing from fear to confusion and sometimes to bliss. During this stage you will be in a deep state of consciousness and you may experience a deep sense of your inner nature, and identification with a force greater than yourself.

Some degree of fear is quite a common experience in transition – you may feel that your body will be torn apart by the baby, or even that you could die. It is thought that this fear may have a useful function in that it makes your body secrete adrenalin. Whereas in the first stage adrenalin hinders the processes of labour, in the second stage it could act as a necessary trigger for the expulsive work of the uterus.

Although not everyone has these feelings in transition, they are common enough that it is worth you knowing about them beforehand. This will prevent you being overwhelmed by them, and you can take them as a sign that you have nearly completed the first (and probably longest) part of labour.

Positions in Transition

In transition there are so many conflicting sensations in your body that you may have to try a number of different positions before you find one that suits you. A lot of women find the kneeling position supported by cushions or their partner most comfortable. The feelings of restlessness and of not being able to cope any longer that characterize this stage of labour are sometimes best handled by changing positions every so often.

Forearms supported on a chair or a pillow
A good way to achieve a 'dynamic resting state'. You can rest your head in this position.

Breathing in Transition

Because of the intensity of the contractions at this stage, you will probably find that your breathing will become shallower and more rapid during contractions. You need to let this happen but in between contractions, remember to return to your slow, deep breathing. Both whispered ah and puffy cheek breathing focus on breathing out, helping you to stay calm, and allowing the final part of the dilatation of the cervix.

Anterior Lip

Sometimes you may get the urge to push before your cervix is fully dilated, that is, when there is still a rim of cervix left that has not been fully pulled up into the uterus. This is referred to as an 'anterior lip' and your midwife will ask you to resist the urge to push because pushing at this point makes the 'lip' swell up and stop dilating effectively. The urge to push can be very strong and not something a woman feels she can control. As one woman said, 'They might as well have asked me to hold a huge tidal wave back with my hands!'

You can use your breathing to help resist the urge to push. Try breathing only with the upper part of the chest and breathe two short in-and-out breaths, ending with a gentle blowing out: 'huff, huff, blow'. Keep repeating this breathing for as long as the urge to push is there. When the contraction wears off, go back to slow, slightly deeper, breathing.

Another way of resisting the urge to push is to get into the knee-chest position (see below), with your head down and bottom up in the air. Adopting this position, while exhaling slowly during contractions, takes the pressure of the baby's head off the cervix and allows the cervix to dilate completely.

Once the lip is out of the way you are ready to go!

'As I got to the end of the first stage it all started to seem a bit unreal. I was in monkey and I thought that if I could only stand up really straight this whole thing would just be an illusion and I could walk out of there. But then the pushing urge started and as there was a "lip" I wasn't allowed to go with the push. I spent quite some time on the bed with my bottom in the air and head down trying to breathe "huff, huff, blow". At one time there were five other people in the room, all encouraging me by going "huff, huff, blow" as well. What a sight it must have been. I actually thought it was quite funny, especially when I couldn't resist the urge to push and went "huff, huff, aaargh!"' *Kate*

Knee-chest position
This reduces the pressure of the baby's head on the cervix and is therefore an extremely useful position to adopt during transition if there is an anterior lip.

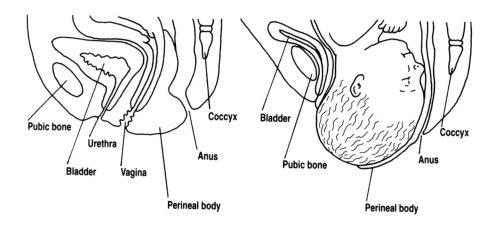

The perineal body is a pyramid-shaped wedge of muscle fibres, the base of which is called the perineum. To allow the baby to pass through, the perineal body flattens out; from being about 4cm by 4cm it becomes thin and almost transparent with a length of about 10cm.

At the birth, the bladder is drawn up into the abdomen, the rectum is compressed, the vagina is distended and the perineal body is flattened and thinned out.

Second Stage

The second stage of labour is the time from when the cervix is fully dilated until the birth of the baby. The nature of the contractions changes from the first stage; instead of contracting in order to open up the cervix, they become expulsive. During each contraction, the uterus rears forwards, away from the spine, and the force of the contraction is transmitted through the baby's spine, pushing her down through the birth canal. When the head reaches the pelvic floor and distends it, this triggers off the urge to push, and the involuntary expulsive action of the abdominal muscles also comes into play, to assist the work of the uterus.

Many women enjoy this stage, especially if they have had a long transition. The mother is over the long hard struggle and knows that soon she will have completed perhaps the greatest feat of her life. It feels more purposeful, and she is completely engrossed in her work. These pushing contractions feel more 'muscular' than in the first stage – they build up with a tremendous power that is totally involuntary. If you can go with them and not resist, they can be pleasurable.

In order to be born, the baby must negotiate the mother's pelvis. The inlet to the pelvis is oval shaped, with the long axis lying from side to side and so, because the baby's head is longest from front to back, it enters the pelvis with the back towards one side, and the brow to the other. However, the longest axis of the pelvic outlet is from the front to the back, i.e., from the pubic bone to the coccyx – so in order to be born her head has to rotate forwards, in the pelvic cavity, until the back of her head is directly in line with the pubic bone. This is effected by the expulsive contractions pushing the baby's head against the pelvic floor, which, being gutter shaped, directs the back of the baby's head (or whichever part is leading – in a breech birth the baby's bottom, and in some cases the baby's face) towards the front.

The baby's body, of course, has to perform a similar manoeuvre. The baby's shoulders enter the pelvis lying diagonally across the pelvic inlet. As the body moves down in the pelvic cavity and meets the pelvic floor, the front shoulder rotates forwards until it lies next to the pubic bone and the back shoulder is next to the coccyx. From this position, with a sideways bending of the body to conform to the shape of the birth canal, first the front shoulder, then the back shoulder are born.

'I love that feeling just as the baby is born. It's hard to describe but there's the most wonderful sensation inside my whole body right from the top of my head. Complete happiness. I could do it again just for that!'
Gaynor, mother of three

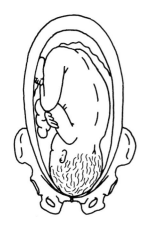  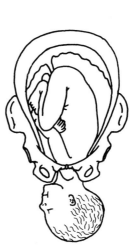

The manner in which the baby negotiates the mother's pelvis in the second stage of labour is an example of how well a woman's body is designed for childbirth.

Positions in Second Stage

Positions where the woman is more upright, such as kneeling, squatting, monkey, lunging or on all fours all help the descent of the baby.

Squatting is ideal for the actual delivery. However, if you have not learned to squat well and comfortably before you go into labour, there is a slight risk of straining muscles and ligaments, which you might not notice at the time because you are so engrossed in the labour. Supported squatting is an excellent alternative. You can take support either from furniture or fixtures, or from your birth supporter. Being supported makes it much easier to release your hip joints and let your knees go away from each other. The pelvic floor is then able to release more effectively, allowing the force of the contraction to push the baby through the birth canal. If, for any reason, you need to speed up the second stage, squatting is the position to adopt. This is preferable to what could turn out to be a forceps delivery.

In some situations lying on the side is appropriate. Though the force of gravity will not be assisting the birth, if the baby is descending well from the strength of the contractions this will not matter; and though the pelvis does not have complete mobility in this position, it is possible for the sacrum to move out of the way. It is a safe position in that you are not putting the weight of the baby on the inferior major blood vessel returning blood to the heart.

Women who are giving birth in a half-sitting, half-lying-down position will commonly pull their heads back strongly, almost in an attempt to get away from the sensations, which makes them push less effectively. Some midwives will advise you to tuck your chin down on to your chest. It is better to have support behind your head and neck, from your partner or from cushions, and if possible try not to pull your head back .

Going with the Spontaneous Urge to Push

Many women find that once they are fully dilated the contractions subside for a while before the second stage starts in earnest. This is thought to be physiological, and allows a well-earned rest. The expulsive contractions of the second stage, which push the baby down the birth canal, are often slightly further apart than in the first stage, giving you time to collect yourself. When the baby's head reaches the pelvic floor and presses against it, an involuntary urge to push is stimulated. In many labours the woman is told to push, with monumental effort, before she really feels she wants to. However, it is now recognized that it can in fact be counter-productive for a woman to push in this way, and is not a natural part of the birth process.

Pushing too soon and too hard frequently means that the woman over-exerts herself, causing unnecessary stress and strain to both herself and the baby. Typically, what happens when a woman is told to push is that she holds her breath. This causes the throat to close, the abdominals and the ribcage muscles to tense, the diaphragm to be lowered and held, and the pelvic floor to tense. When you push in this way, what you are actually doing is pushing down further with the diaphragm, which raises the pressure inside the chest cavity and compresses the large veins returning blood to the heart. The output from the heart falls, blood pressure drops, and in a very short time the baby will be receiving less oxygen and his heart rate will have fallen.

During this pushing stage the baby's head slips back a little between each contraction. Prolonged breath-holding will make you suddenly gasp for air as you can no longer hold back, and can set off a suction pull which will make the baby's head slip back even further. Almost a case of two steps forwards and three steps back!

Prolonged breath-holding also not only puts great stress on the abdominal muscles and can lead to separation of these muscles, but it also strains the ligaments that hold the pelvic organs in place. You also increase the risk of tearing as you are trying to push through a tense pelvic floor. This is definitely not the easiest way to give birth!

It is a different story if a woman is allowed to trust her own experience of the birth; when you have the overwhelming and irresistible desire to push, you should simply join in with the spontaneous urge of your body. Once the baby's head is firmly on the pelvic floor, you will feel this urge to push most strongly at the height of the contraction – in fact there are often several natural 'pushes' in each contraction.

When you follow your body's urge to push, the breath is forcibly exhaled as the ribcage moves in. The diaphragm rises, and the abdominal muscles contract, decreasing the space in the abdominal cavity and assisting the expulsive contractions of the uterus. A distinctive 'grunting' is often a sign of natural spontaneous pushing, as the woman instinctively slows down the out-breath, making the diaphragm rise more slowly, and the contraction of the abdominals slower. A powerful contraction where the involuntary squeeze is not mediated by an out-breath can be overwhelming in its intensity, and leave the woman gasping for breath.

During the contractions, therefore, it is advisable that you focus your attention on letting the breath out slowly and fully (which also ensures a full in-breath). Making a noise is also extremely effective – but make sure that you keep the sound low, such as grunting and bellowing. High-pitched screaming not only tires you out, but also tightens the throat and facial muscles, and consequently causes tension in the pelvic floor.

The more relaxed all the muscles of your body are at this stage the easier the birth will be. The key here is to be able to co-ordinate the abdominal muscles giving help to the uterus in pushing the baby out, while staying relaxed in the legs, face and jaw, so that the pelvic floor can release. Puffy cheek breathing and whispered ah on the out-breath are again particularly useful for this as they release tension in the jaw and mouth.

There are some circumstances when you do have actively to push with contractions whether you feel ready to or not, for example if you have a big baby, or if she is lying in a difficult position, or you need to get her out quickly because of her condition; if you do, then remember to take a good in-breath as the contraction starts, then slowly exhale on a whispered ah, contracting your abdominal muscles strongly with the out-breath. At the same time, think of directing the push down into your bottom, and releasing your pelvic floor. Remember not to hold your breath and that several short pushes can be just as effective as one long one. You should also try deep or supported squatting, which is one of the best ways to speed up the second stage.

Breathing the Baby Out

Once the back of the baby's head has extended from behind the pubic bone it no longer slips back up the birth canal between contractions. This is called 'crowning' and you will now be able to see the top of your baby's head at your vagina. The stretch put on the perineum causes a burning sensation a bit like pulling your mouth open with your fingers, then it will feel numb. It is absolutely vital that you do not force the moment of birth, because this could cause tearing. Rather, you should stay calm and controlled to allow the baby to emerge into the world gradually and gently. You need to stop the extra pushing exerted by the abdominals, and allow the uterus alone to give those few last pushes that will enable your baby to be born. 'Not pushing' is very hard if you have good expulsive contractions, and some women will simply surrender to the force. To avoid pushing, try breathing in a rapid, light panting fashion which reduces the strength of the abdominal contractions, and lets the uterus 'nudge' the baby out. If the contractions are not so strong you can simply breathe the baby out using a whispered ah and directing the breath into your perineum.

Your baby is born! The midwife will hand you the baby and you can sit back, place her on your breast and look at her for the first time. Directly at birth your baby may look very slightly bluish and lacking in tone, but as she starts breathing this will bring a healthy colour and vitality to her body. The top of the head might look pointed or the face a little squashed as the proportionately large head has moulded itself on the way through the passage of the birth canal. Newborn babies often look a bit wrinkled and they are covered in a creamy white coating called vernix. Even if there is also some blood on her it is better not to wash her as the vernix gives her protection from the change in temperature and provides nourishment through the skin. A newborn baby's senses can be very alert and she will be as full of the wonders of life as you are at this moment.

Third Stage

However, labour is not completely over yet, as the third stage, when the uterus expels the placenta, is still to come. The placenta (or afterbirth) is a round, flat organ about 15–20cm in diameter, and 3cm thick. It is made up of blood vessels that supply the mother's blood with its nutrients and oxygen to the baby, and carry the baby's blood containing carbon dioxide and other waste products back to the mother. After the baby is delivered, the uterus continues to contract, causing the placenta to come away from the wall of the uterus, and to be expelled from the mother.

While you are waiting for the placenta to be delivered you can get to know your baby. The baby's suckling reflex is very strong immediately after the birth and if you put her to the breast she will probably take your nipple straight away. The sensation of the baby sucking, or even just the contact with your breast or nipple, increases the secretion of the hormone oxytocin (see page 123) in the mother which makes the contractions stronger.

It has become a fairly common practice to give the mother an injection of syntometrine to induce the uterus to contract at this stage, to prevent haemorrhage. It is also common to cut the cord immediately after delivery of the baby. Neither of these practices is strictly necessary. Unless there are signs of excessive bleeding or if the mother has had an epidural, making it harder for the uterus to contract, the placenta will be expelled naturally within an hour of the birth. The cord will naturally stop pulsating after the birth, which would be the logical time to cut it. While the placenta is still attached to the mother and the cord pulsating, the baby is receiving oxygen, which safeguards her, especially if there have been complications or she has been distressed.

Squatting or monkey are good positions in which to deliver the placenta. It is only about a sixth of the weight of the baby, and is soft and slippery, so it is much easier to deliver and it can be a pleasurable sensation. The midwife will examine the placenta to make sure that it has come out intact and no part of it is left inside the uterus, as this could cause infection. Having taken the time to expel the placenta spontaneously, the labour and birth has come to a natural end, leaving the mother with a sense of accomplishment and satisfaction.

9 Overcoming Fear and Pain in Labour

However much you have prepared yourself for birth, it is only natural to feel anxiety about it. It is an unavoidable event that has of necessity to come at the end of pregnancy. First-time mothers fear the 'unknown' they are about to experience, and fear the pain they have heard they will have to endure. It is undeniable that, in labour, the over-riding stimuli most women have to deal with are the stresses of fear and pain.

Contractions

Although it is an unknown experience that you are facing, it is helpful to try not to pre-judge what the sensations of the contractions will be like. The word 'pain' is sometimes used synonymously with 'contractions', which does not help our attitudes towards labour as we still do not have any idea of the degree of pain, or of the quality. It would be helpful if there were another word in our vocabulary specifically for the 'pain' experienced in labour.

The sensation of a contraction is hard to describe. Most women will tell you that it is not like any other pain. It usually builds up with the contraction, reaches a peak and then disperses quickly, being felt as a 'wave'. Most women describe how the contraction starts at the top of the uterus and radiates downwards, being experienced most strongly at the cervix. The pain results from the nerve fibres in the uterus being stimulated as the muscle fibres contract. It is felt most strongly at the cervix and the lower segment of the uterus because these fibres are stretching and retracting to enable the cervix to open. Pain may also be experienced as the pelvic ligaments and soft tissues stretch, and as the contracting uterus exerts pressure on the other pelvic organs and the joints. Between contractions the pain usually goes completely.

Many women experience the contraction not as a pain arising from illness or injury but as a 'functional' pain, as it is your uterus performing its physiological function of expelling the baby out into the world. If a woman can label the pain of contractions in this way, she is much more likely to deal with the experience positively, allowing it to 'happen' more, instead of being anxious and resisting, thus hindering the physiological processes of the birth.

Common Reflex Responses to Fear and Pain

The common reaction to fear and pain, in our everyday lives and in labour, is to tense our muscles in ways that harmfully affect our use. The characteristic reaction to fear is what is called the 'startle pattern'. This is a neuromuscular response in which a wave of contraction passes through the body. An example of this is when people respond to a sudden loud noise – they contract their neck muscles, pull their heads back, hunch their shoulders and hold their arms stiffly at the sides, with a flattened chest and bent knees.

Our normal response to pain is the 'flexor reflex', which involves contracting our flexor muscles, and which in many situations serves a useful purpose in that it allows us to move the body part away from the cause of pain – quickly. For example, if you step on something sharp you immediately pull the leg up under you; similarly, if you prick your hand on a pin you flex your arm muscles to withdraw the hand and arm. In childbirth it is the flexor reflex response to pain in the abdomen that is at work, urging the woman to crouch down over the pain, the body bending forwards and the knees drawn up towards the stomach.

In labour women commonly react to the pain of contractions with a combination of these two reflex patterns, or they may have a 'pet area' that they habitually tighten in response to stress in their everyday lives. This creates a tension in our musculature that is the opposite of that which we work to achieve in Alexander lessons. If you use the Alexander skills of muscular inhibition and direction and avoid tensing in response to the pain, you will almost certainly have a better labour.

Women who have been practising the Alexander Technique for some time will have helped themselves by releasing some of their chronic muscular tension, thus increasing their ability to cope with stress and giving them greater confidence before they go into labour. Basically, the more confident you can feel about your ability to give birth and cope with the pain, the less likely you are to go into this stereotyped fear response and create the very situation you are fearing. Pain is felt more acutely when muscles, particularly those in the neck, are tensed, and it is quite possible to go into a vicious circle of pain producing fear which creates increased tension which leads to increased perception of pain.

If you are able to maintain this state of relaxed balance in the musculature, it is also less likely that you will react to the stresses of childbirth by going into the 'fight or flight' mechanism. This is a primitive defence reaction that is activated by fear, anxiety or anger, and is the body's way of preparing itself for an emergency. It involves the interaction between the brain, the nervous system and a variety of different hormones, and is interesting in that it is a very clear demonstration of the basic unity of body and mind. The hormone adrenalin is secreted, the heart rate increases, the blood pressure goes up, the breathing rate becomes more rapid so that more oxygen is available, the liver releases sugar into the blood for quick energy, the blood is diverted to the heart, lungs and skeletal muscles, and tension in the muscles increases. All these physiological changes happen so that we have strength and energy easily available to cope with the emergency, and they are healthy, so long as we either 'fight or flee'.

Unfortunately there are some negative aspects to this response – especially when it occurs in labour. The muscles tense up in preparation for action, but if we do not do anything with this extra energy it becomes locked into the muscles as tension. Excessive tension, as we have already seen, tends to heighten our perception of the pain and is harmful to our overall use and functioning, so in labour the most beneficial thing to do is to keep inhibiting any tensing in those common tension areas, especially the neck, and translate the extra energy that goes into the muscles into movement (the Alexander procedures).

Another of the detrimental effects of this response is that, as the blood is directed to the skeletal muscles, heart and lungs, the blood supply to the digestive organs and uterus is reduced, thus denying the uterus the energy it needs to push the baby out.

In addition, the release of adrenalin into the body causes the circular fibres that run around the cervix to contract which has the effect of closing the cervix. However, at the same time the longitudinal and oblique muscles of the cervix are retracting and shortening, trying to open the cervix, and the subsequent antagonistic pulls of the muscles can be painful.

Nature's Painkillers

Endorphins are the hormones and chemicals that cause us to feel a sense of well-being and pleasure, and also act as our bodies' natural painkillers. (One of them is said to be two hundred times more powerful in analgesic effect than morphine.) The flow of endorphins can be stimulated in a variety of ways – rhythmic movements including jogging, dancing, singing, being gently stroked, meditation, relaxation, laughing and orgasm.

In pregnant women the pituitary gland, which releases endorphins, develops an extra lobe, and the level of endorphins in their blood can be up to eight times the normal level. Endorphins diffuse through the placenta and consequently the foetus also has a very high level of endorphins. During pregnancy endorphins facilitate secretion of the hormone prolactin, which completes the maturing process of the baby's lungs. (Prolactin is also the breastfeeding hormone; after birth endorphins act to release this hormone.)

Both mother and baby retain high levels of endorphins for about an hour after the birth. It is thought that the effect of this is the physiological basis for 'bonding' between mother and baby. One study shows that babies only one week old can recognize their mother's scent and will turn towards their own mother's breast pads. The stimulation from the scent releases endorphins in the baby.

In active labour, endorphins and the hormone oxytocin are released to produce a natural analgesia. (Oxytocin is the hormone that makes the uterus contract in labour. Interestingly, oxytocin also stimulates the uterine contractions that occur during orgasm – not surprisingly, it is often called the happiness hormone.) As the pain increases during labour the production of oxytocin and endorphins also increases, and as a result women in labour often appear to be in a different state of consciousness, almost a state of trance, with no normal sense of time. In this state the woman is better able to cope with the pain of contractions, experiencing harmony between mind and body. Although the exact basis of this state is not known, it is firmly believed that it is facilitated by the secretions of endorphins.

However, if a woman is anxious and fearful during labour, the adrenalin-type hormones mentioned earlier inhibit both the process of labour and prevent the release of endorphins. This increases the pain of labour. When conditions are right, though, when the woman can feel confident and secure and stay calm, the supply of endorphins will remain constant. Towards the end of labour, this supply tapers off and it is thought that at this time the body deliberately produces adrenalin-type hormones which help stimulate the pushing contractions of the second stage of labour.

Common Tension Patterns

The way someone habitually responds to stressful situations is likely to be the way they respond in labour, but in labour it will be intensified. As a preparation for labour, it is useful to notice your habitual muscular response when confronted with anxiety and pain, and practise inhibiting and giving your directions to maintain good use. You do not have to set up fearful and painful situations deliberately – for most of us there are enough stressful situations that occur spontaneously in our everyday life. For example, because hospitals are unfamiliar environments for most of us, it is quite common for women find that their antenatal appointments are a slightly stressful experience; this is a good opportunity for you to notice how you respond.

Other habitual muscular patterns will also show up. If, for instance, we have a habit of holding our breath and tensing our muscles when concentrating or during hard work, then that is almost certainly going to be our response to the effort of labour. If we can become aware of these habits, and practise inhibition and direction when we are pregnant, then it will be easier to respond in this way in labour.

We will look in more detail at specific tension patterns that commonly occur in labour, and give you some ideas on how to release these. You should always bear in mind that no part of the body works in isolation, and remember to come back to your primary directions.

You will also find that all these common tension areas respond very well to having your partner or midwife putting a gentle hand on them. If you are tensing up strongly it becomes more difficult to notice for yourself, but the contact of a relaxed hand can help bring your attention to the area. Sometimes in labour a hard, firm pressure is what is needed, but often a gentle touch with an open hand, not gripping or interfering, can communicate reassurance and help you to release unnecessary tension more effectively.

The Neck

In labour, and indeed in every moment of our lives, the most commonly tightened area of the body is in the muscles of the neck. These form the most important muscle group in the whole of our body as regards our use and movement, and any tensing of them will cause a contraction of muscles throughout the body. For this reason, this is the first place where tension should be released. You may be able to use inhibition and directions to keep your neck free, but if you find this too difficult use the whispered ah, vocalizing, or movement in the monkey, squat, lunge, or all fours as a way of releasing tension.

The Face

Frowning and tightening the jaw and mouth is a common reaction to pain. The muscles of the face and jaw are very closely related to the muscles of the neck and when we frown and tighten the jaw and mouth we also tense the neck. There are also many muscles on the scalp that we tend to tighten when in pain. Try concentrating hard on something and you will probably notice that you do this to some extent.

Becoming aware of this very common habit and learning to keep your face, jaw and mouth soft helps you to keep your neck free from unnecessary tension. Keeping your eyes focused and alert, and directing your neck to be free, will help you stay relaxed and calm in the muscles of the face and head.

The whispered ah and puffy cheek breathing are the best and easiest ways to release tension in the face and neck. Remember that the amount of tension in the mouth is directly linked to the amount of tension in the vagina and the pelvic floor.

The Shoulders

The shoulders are very often the area that is tightened when under stress. When you tense your shoulders the neck muscles also tense up. Explore this by pulling your shoulders up and noticing what happens to your neck and the effect this has on your breathing. You will find that you have pulled your head and neck down between your shoulders at the same time and that breathing becomes more difficult because you have restricted the free play of the ribcage.

Asking the neck muscles to release, letting the shoulders drop and allowing the arms to hang freely at your sides will help your back to lengthen and widen and give you free movement in the ribcage.

In the monkey, squat and lunge, because the torso is inclined forwards the arms hang freely and this helps to release tension in the shoulders. Gently rocking or circling in these positions is also helpful.

Notice that as you release your shoulders your breathing becomes freer and deeper.

The Arms

Women often clench their hands extremely hard during contractions. This causes tension in the shoulders, face and neck. Make a fist with your hand and tighten your whole arm. Feel what happens in the rest of your body. Notice how this pulls the arm inwards towards the side of your body, which restricts your breathing. Notice also how your neck and shoulders tense and how your lower back tightens.

To help release your arms you need to remember that they hang from the shoulder girdle, which is supported by the spine. So think about keeping a good head/neck/back relationship, and release down the length of the arm and out through the fingertips. Remember to keep the hands open and relaxed, and to think about having a lot of space and freedom in the shoulder, elbow and wrist joints.

An image of water flowing down through the length of the arm may be helpful. You can also combine this with the whispered ah, thinking of 'sending' the breath down the arms and out through the fingertips.

The Abdominal Muscles

The cramp-like sensations of contractions can make a woman want to crouch down over the pain, which involves tensing the abdominal muscles. Try contracting your abdominal muscles quite hard, and notice how this pulls your chest down and rounds your spine forwards, and also how it affects your breathing – you will find that you are breathing into your upper chest only. You may also notice that your pelvic floor tenses. Release your abdominal muscles and you will notice how the chest comes up again, in a similar way to when the restraint is taken off a spring and it bounces up. This allows the expansion of the whole ribcage, which is necessary for healthy breathing. Notice also how the pelvic floor releases.

Rather than scrunching yourself forwards, think of keeping a good head/neck/back relationship, or go into one of the procedures (monkey, etc.) that encourage this alignment of the spine. Practising the whispered ah is also effective in releasing tension here, as it encourages the slow contraction and then full release of the abdominals.

Released and soft abdominals will allow the unrestricted and deep breathing that will help you to stay calm and confident. With every contraction the uterus tips forwards slightly, and your abdominals need to be relaxed so that they don't restrain this movement. In the second stage they play an important role in assisting the expulsion of the baby, and over-tense muscles will work less well.

The Small of the Back

We have seen that it is a common habit in most people to over-contract muscles in the small of the back, and this is equally true in labour. Tension in the neck muscles makes this area tighten, as does the pain caused by the baby's head pressing hard against the inside of the sacrum as it descends through the birth canal.

In lessons we work to release tension throughout the length of the spine and the teacher often puts a hand on the lower back, encouraging you to lengthen down the whole of the back. This is what you have to do here.

The monkey (or any variation of monkey), perhaps making use of the support of your partner or leaning against a wall or piece of furniture, is especially helpful for releasing tension in the lower back. Also try gently rocking while in these positions.

You may find it useful to think of having a long, heavy tail – like a lion tail – reaching all the way down to the floor. This sense of the back continuing all the way to the floor helps you to release the tightening in the lower back.

The Knees and Legs

When the baby's head starts to descend through the birth canal there is often a strong unconscious tendency to pull the knees together. If you tighten your thigh muscles and pull the knees together when standing you will notice that your pelvic floor muscles tense up; your buttocks and lower back muscles may also tighten, disturbing your balance.

The less we interfere with the primary control, the freer the legs become. To release tightening in the inner thigh you must think firstly of maintaining a good head/neck/back relationship and then let the knees to go forwards and away. Monkey, squatting and lunging all encourage this release.

As with tension in the arms, it helps to imagine water flowing down your spine, down through the legs and out through the soles of your feet. Or you can try imagining that the breath of a whispered ah is going through your body, down your legs, and out through your feet. This releases tension away from the centre of the body – away and out of the body.

Often women find it helpful to have someone simply putting a soft hand on the inside of the knees or gently stroking the thighs. If you are in monkey your partner or birth attendant can also help by gently stroking down the back of the thighs. Releasing tension in the inner thigh will help you to release the pelvic floor, and also free up your breathing.

'Being in the water gave support and made it easier to release. I was really aware of letting go all the time. Chanting helped me relax the upper part of my chest, face and neck, and I was imagining that this was connected to my pelvis so that by relaxing one I was relaxing the other. Sometimes my legs started shaking so I would think "OK, relax." I would stretch my legs out occasionally or take my knees up underneath me. The midwife massaged my legs, behind my knees and my back, which was really good.' *Beverly*

---

10 | Birth Support

One of the most important factors in having a successful, happy birth is the emotional support the mother receives during the labour. That support can come from the baby's father, the midwife, a close friend or relative, or the doctors – ideally it is a combination.

The Role of the Father

Until quite recently in the Western world, men were excluded from the birth, and we have the stereotypical image of the expectant father pacing the corridors of the hospital, or waiting downstairs at home boiling up pots of water. Men are now encouraged to be at the birth. However, particularly in a hospital setting, this has not meant that the father has begun participating in a meaningful way. Very often men feel inadequate; their partner is in pain and they want to help, but they just don't know how. They may also feel superfluous; it is a woman's experience and they can feel excluded by the women there. There are some midwives who treat the fathers rather patronizingly, and doctors can also be intimidating. No longer on his home ground, the man does not feel he has a say in what is happening to his partner.

This is a great tragedy. He may be the one person that a woman can trust at this time, who can encourage and guide her, and give her the confidence that she needs. Men who have shared this experience of their baby being born nearly always say that it was one of the most wonderful experiences of their lives. It can bring new depths of love and understanding to the couple's relationship and definitely affects positively the future relationship with the child.

Of course, just as there were men in the past who wanted to be at the birth against the prevailing attitudes, there are nowadays men who do not want to be, and women who do not want their men to be present. It must be up to each couple to choose their own arrangement, without feeling any pressure to conform to something that has become more common.

Although a very beautiful birth experience may happen spontaneously, as with many other areas of our lives a little forethought and preparation does make this outcome considerably more likely. It obviously helps if the father learns as much about what actually happens at the birth before the labour. What is most beneficial is finding ways in which the father is able to be involved and to help during the labour.

Ideally, lessons for pregnancy and childbirth should not be only for the expectant mother, but also for the expectant father.

If your partner comes to some of your Alexander lessons with you he can learn the movements and positions for the birth. He may then be able to make practical suggestions during labour if you are unable to find a useful position for yourself. He can also learn how to look after his own use, so that he does not strain himself and so that he can provide the best physical support for his partner. (Monkey and lunge are best; see pages 36 and 38.)

For the woman being supported to feel comfortable it is extremely important that her partner also feels comfortable. It is not just a matter of supporting the woman's weight – she will also have the downward thrust of the contraction going through her body, and the force may be tremendously strong. If her supporter is stiffening up and straining, that will immediately be communicated to the mother; she will not trust the support and will stiffen in turn. Wherever the supporter can make things easier for himself, he should do so. Sitting on a chair, using cushions, leaning against a wall, counterbalancing his weight with his partner's, are all ways of having to do less work.

Practising these supported positions also increases the couple's trust and communication. They learn to be trusting and adept in handling each other and it is a marvellous chance to work through a lot of fears and misunderstandings before the birth. During labour, because of the intense stimulation from the contracting uterus, women are highly sensitive to how they are touched. Sometimes they want a lot of support and contact, at other times they do not want to be touched at all. The supporter should be aware of this possibility, and it should be discussed beforehand so that he does not take her refusal as a rejection. This may sound unnecessary, but emotions are running very high in a labour and it is very easy for the father to be upset. It goes without saying that the better communication and trust there is in the relationship the better they will cope with whatever comes up during birth.

The Role of the Alexander Teacher

If you do not have an established relationship with the midwife it is helpful to have a further birth-support person and this is where your teacher could help. Sometimes fathers can be rather emotionally distraught and it does help to have someone present who is not so emotionally involved. Also, if you are intending to use positions involving your partner giving physical support, he may be pleased of the extra help. Sometimes the baby's father seems more exhausted than the mother after an active birth!

Some Alexander teachers will accompany you to the baby's birth as your birth support, and this can be enormously helpful. The whole focus of an Alexander teacher's work is the ability to see how a person creates unnecessary tension in response to whatever is happening, and to facilitate the best use of the body so that it functions at its best. These are excellent skills for a birth attendant to have at a labour. She should be able to help minimize unnecessary tension by putting her hands on you, but of course during labour you may not be thinking of inhibiting and directing. However, we have found that someone who has had lessons will know how to respond to the stimulus of the teacher's touch; women in labour are incredibly sensitive to Alexander work.

A vivid illustration of the Alexander teacher's role during labour is given by Dr Dorothy Drew, an obstetric and gynaecological consultant, who herself trained as an Alexander teacher in the 1940s.

In the labour she describes, everything went well for the first six hours, until midday, but by evening the dilation had not increased, the foetal heart rate was irregular and the woman was becoming exhausted. One of Alexander's assistants happened to be staying with Dr Drew and offered to come in and help. The teacher was able to counteract the woman's tendency to "screw herself up and throw herself about and interfere with the uterine action instinctively". The effect was that the contractions came less frequently and became more effective, the baby's heart became regular again and the cervix dilated satisfactorily. From then on labour progressed without further problems, and when the baby was born, twenty-four hours later, the woman's condition was much better than it had been when the teacher was called in. Dr Drew's explanation of the effect of the Alexander Technique was that: "The tensions that she [the patient] put in were undone for her – that is the only way I can put it – so that the uterus could work uninterrupted by the muscular spasms she was putting in."

PART FOUR
The Alexander Technique for Parenting

11 | After the Baby Is Born

Nothing changes you quite so much as becoming a mother. And if this is your first baby your lifestyle will never be the same again. When you are pregnant the emphasis in antenatal classes, books and interest from family and friends is very much focused on the birth and the expected baby. Few think to prepare women for the period immediately after the birth, when life changes dramatically and the mother has to adjust physically and mentally to her new role. How you care for yourself after the birth – both emotionally and physically – will affect you for the rest of your life, so it is worth trying to be as aware of the potential pitfalls as possible.

Alexander Can Help
After the relatively long and slow process of pregnancy, the labour and birth are extremely intense and dramatic events. Directly afterwards you may feel disorientated, tired, tender and often fragile and vulnerable. The tremendously hard work of giving birth can make you feel as if everything you learned in your Alexander education has been completely forgotten, but the knowledge will still be there, and it can easily be brought back to conscious awareness.

For most women a gentle Alexander lesson is enough to remind them of their directions and to help them re-experience the working of the primary control. Just having gentle hands on your head, neck, back and shoulders can help you to become aware of your own body again. With a newborn baby to care for, it can seem difficult to fit in a lesson. We suggest that you have one as soon as you feel strong enough. Some teachers will see both you and your baby, and if you do not feel up to travelling for the first few weeks a teacher may be prepared to visit you at home.

It is important to use your body as well as possible right from the beginning of your mothering role, as it is now that the habits connected with childcare activities will be established. Softened ligaments and muscles will still be vulnerable at this stage, so avoid over-straining, which may cause long-term damage. The increased awareness of yourself that you acquire through Alexander lessons can help alert you to the signs of misuse so that you can do something about it before it becomes habitual. If you are having lessons now you can ask your teacher to go through some of the things suggested in this section with you.

Reclaiming Your Body and Sense of Self

The accepted image of motherhood, painted by the media, family and friends, is of something completely wonderful. However, caring for the newborn baby is one of the most demanding and unrelenting tasks you will ever undertake. However much you love your child and your new role as a mother, it is, nevertheless, a time of great physical as well as intense emotional demands. The immediacy of having to care for the baby means that the mother puts the baby's needs first and her own second. Through ignoring her own needs the mother may start to feel tired and resentful towards the baby, which in turn leads to feelings of guilt and inadequacy as a mother. Being a new mother can very often feel much less than wonderful!

The increased sensory awareness that you acquire through the Alexander Technique gives you a stronger sense of self; this will be invaluable in the period shortly after the baby is born, although it can be difficult to maintain. A woman who has undergone labour and birth with support from her partner and midwife, who has been treated respectfully and who has been kept informed and aware of events during all the stages, will have more of a sense of being in control of her own body. It will be easier for her to recover her sense of self. But if she has had a difficult birth with a lot of medical intervention, she may feel alienated and a stranger to her own body. Alexander lessons can give you the opportunity to release the shock of the birth, as well as the emotions that often well up afterwards.

Many new mothers feel more feminine, more in touch with their feelings than before, and actually like their new softness and roundness. The close loving contact with the baby during breastfeeding can also be very pleasurable, sensual and reaffirming. For some women it can be the first time in their lives when they feel a complete acceptance of themselves.

However, many women do not like their bodies at all at this time, feeling plump, flabby, in pain and as if they belonged to the baby instead of to themselves. It is quite likely that sometimes you will feel good about yourself and at others you will not enjoy your body at all, or perhaps a contradictory mixture of both views.

Giving your Alexander directions can help you to find a focal point, a sense of inner stillness, when you feel overwhelmed by all these contrasting and perhaps conflicting emotions. It gives you a sense of your self that is independent of your moods and your situation.

In Alexander's fourth book, *The Universal Constant in Living*, he quotes Shakespeare: 'To thine own self be true; and it must follow, as the night the day, thou canst not then be false to any man'. Alexander says that 'knowing oneself' is part and parcel of the process of learning the Alexander Technique, and that the increased recognition of responsibility for your own self will lead to an understanding and consideration of others and their well-being. Applied to the mother–baby relationship, if the mother has a healthy sense of her own self and is able to get her own needs met, she will then be better able to love and care for her child.

Having a clear sense of self helps you to become aware of your boundaries – of where you end and another person begins; of who you are, and who the other person is. This enables you to have a healthy sense of your psychological separateness from other people – and from your baby. It may seem like a contradiction to talk about being able to separate from the baby at the same time as there being a great emphasis on closeness and bonding. However, if a mother can maintain a healthy sense of separateness from the baby, she can in fact have an even deeper relationship with her child.

If you can learn, right from the beginning, to give yourself the time and space for your own needs, your child will, through your example, learn the 'otherness' of people, which is so essential in any healthy social interaction between people. You will thus be giving your child an invaluable gift for the whole of his or her life.

Getting Back into Shape

Your physical needs are perhaps even greater now, after the birth of your baby, than they were while you were pregnant. Caring for the baby and all the other daily tasks make it difficult to have the necessary rest, and lack of proper rest can aggravate certain physical conditions, like postural imbalances and weak pelvic floors.

Although you may not like to ask for help with housework, this is the best thing that family and friends can do for both you and the baby at this

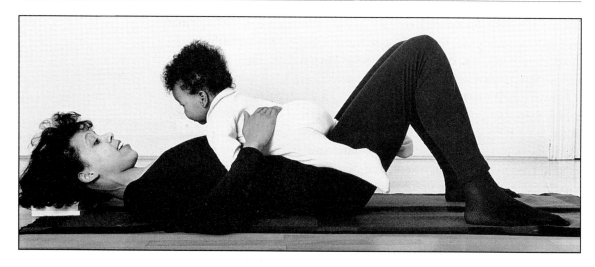

You can relax in semi-supine with your baby lying on your front, and enjoy the closeness and quiet time together.

time. Pregnancy and labour have made great demands on your body, so ideally you should give yourself at least a couple of weeks (or more if you can arrange it) before you take on anything other than directly caring for the baby. Because you are still 'bruised' from the labour, and suffering the effects of broken nights' sleep, rest is vital.

We recommend that you rest lying in semi-supine (see pages 46–50). Try to do this at least once a day for about 20 minutes, or two or three times if possible. This allows the relaxing of unnecessary muscular tension, and will help bring your body back into shape after the stresses of pregnancy.

What is equally important as getting rest is carefully looking after your use. To understand this fully, you need to know about what has happened to you.

While you were pregnant, the physical and hormonal changes were relatively gradual, whereas the body reverts to its pre-pregnant state in a much shorter time. The uterus contracts to its pre-pregnancy size and this takes about six weeks. You will bleed for a few days after the birth, and this will be followed by a discharge which may continue for a couple of weeks. The whole area around the vagina will be engorged and quite tender, especially if you have had stitches. After a couple of days the breasts enlarge and fill with milk. They can feel very sore, and you may experience sensations similar to a period pain when you breastfeed, as the hormone oxytocin causes the uterus to contract.

During the pregnancy you had to adapt to the changing balance caused by carrying the extra weight of the baby. After the baby is born, you have to re-establish good use now that you are no longer carrying the extra weight. Your muscles have stretched a lot and for several weeks your ligaments and muscles will still be soft from the effect of the hormone progesterone.

Having Alexander lessons to reacquire good use and a sense of the primary control functioning will set up the conditions that promote healthy functioning of the musculature as a whole. They will also help you to be more aware of what you are doing to cope with the discomfort of stitches and a sore pelvic floor, or strained ligaments, for this is the kind of situation in which you can easily develop bad habits by setting up compensatory muscular patterns to protect yourself from the pain and discomfort.

The current thinking about damaged and strained ligaments is that they respond best to gentle movement, and that total immobility does not really help. Ligaments are made up of fibres of elastin and collagen. If the ligament is gently stretched during the time it is repairing, the fibres line themselves up, rather like a good darn, producing a strong repair. If a damaged ligament is kept immobile, the fibres will clump together like a bad darn, and although it will repair it will be weak. Rest is important, but so is gentle rhythmic movement such as walking. It does *not* include all the lifting and moving that housework involves!

Many women say that their later-life back problems stem from when they had their first child. Make a conscious choice to prevent future problems by looking after yourself now.

Your Abdominal Muscles After Birth

During pregnancy the abdominal muscles have stretched enormously to accommodate the baby, and they need some special attention if they are going to be able to perform their vital functions adequately in the future. Initially, after the birth, you may not have a lot of sensation if you try to contract or release your abdominals, but a helpful and very gentle way to start to regain control is to do the following exercise.

'Singing who' exercise

This exercise is done standing up. Start by giving your Alexander directions. Place one hand across your lower abdomen (immediately above your pubic bone), and the other above it (it will lie immediately below your ribs).

Now, while maintaining your sense of the head, neck and back in alignment, sing a low 'whoooo' sound. Having your hands on your abdomen while singing your 'who' will help to feel the muscular activity in your abdomen. You will need the help of your Alexander teacher to learn how the out-breath is assisted by the abdominal muscles.

You may feel very self-conscious doing this. However, once you get over that, it is an exercise that most people enjoy tremendously, as it gives you a new awareness of the muscles involved in breathing.

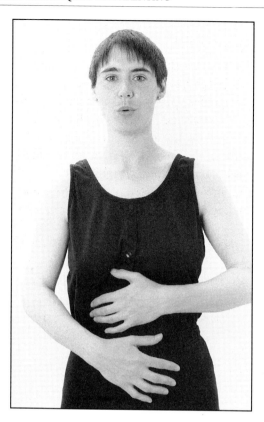

The singing who – a gentle and safe way of regaining the tone in your abdominal muscles.

Voice production is a complex subject beyond the topic of this book; basically, if we are using our voices correctly, the abdominal muscles will be working to provide the breath for speaking. For singing and shouting, our abdominal muscles are called into play more strongly, to provide the increased need for breath. Singing is one way to gently tone up your abdominal muscles – something both you and your baby could enjoy!

In the Alexander Technique we recognize that muscles never work in isolation. As we have already explained, your abdominal muscles are part of the suit of musculature that wraps around the body. All the procedures that we have described – monkey, squatting, the lunge, kneeling and all fours – encourage the lengthening of the muscles of the front of your body as well as the muscles of the back. Therefore, if you are able to use your body well, and apply these procedures to your everyday activities of caring for the baby, your abdominal muscles will be exercised. After the birth of the baby you can work on these with your Alexander teacher, paying special attention to giving you a sense of lengthening up the front. This is another effective and gentle way to start to regain sensation and control of the abdominals. Of course the reality is that with a newborn baby you may not remember or be able to think about how you use yourself all the time. It is an unrealistic expectation. However, the more you do remember to use yourself well, the sooner your abdominal muscles will return to their pre-pregnant state – or better.

In addition to good use in your everyday activities, it is advisable to do some specific abdominal exercises to regain healthy tone (see pages 65–6). The Alexander Technique is not a technique that relies on exercise, but it gives you an awareness of your body use that makes exercising not only safer but also more enjoyable.

Your Pelvic Floor Muscles After Birth

The pelvic floor also needs strengthening after the birth, but because it is not visible it is often ignored. However, it is crucial that pelvic floor exercises are practised so that tone is regained, pelvic organs are supported adequately, and sphincter control is re-established. During the delivery the muscles of the pelvic floor have been stretched immensely. There may be bruising and swelling, and any pressure to the area, whether from outside when sitting and moving, or from inside when lifting, coughing or sneezing, will cause discomfort. In addition, if you have stitches these may be sore for the first few days. All this may make you feel rather reluctant to practise pelvic floor exercises.

Gently contracting and releasing the pelvic floor promotes a better blood flow to the area. This delivers oxygen and nutrients and carries away waste products, thus facilitating the healing process. The improved circulation also alleviates pain caused by haemorrhoids. Muscles that are not exercised waste away, and trying to recover their tone at a later date is even harder than doing it now.

Pelvic floor exercises are a lot easier if you have been practising beforehand because you will be familiar with the muscles and how to isolate and contract them. Pelvic floor contractions should be practised every day, before and after the baby is born – and for the rest of your life. We describe the procedure on page 63.

If after a few weeks you still experience any pain or discomfort in the pelvic floor area, we strongly recommend that you seek medical advice. You know better than your doctor how your body feels, and if you are not reassured by his or her diagnosis you should ask to be referred to a specialist. With the right attitude and motivation it should not be too long before you feel back in shape and able to enjoy normal physical activities and an active sex life.

12 Looking After Your Baby with Good Use

It is important to develop good habits right from the start, since the things you will do every day will have to be done repeatedly over rather a long period of time! If you feel confident and comfortable, all these activities will be more pleasurable for both of you, times when you can communicate with and enjoy each other. By applying Alexander principles, you can also help prevent the development of backache and tension.

Using Your Arms as an Extension of the Back

A common complaint among mothers is tension in the upper arms, shoulders and neck. This is often caused by misuse of the arms while caring for the baby, so before looking at the various new tasks that will be part of your daily life as a mother, it is worth considering how to use your arms efficiently.

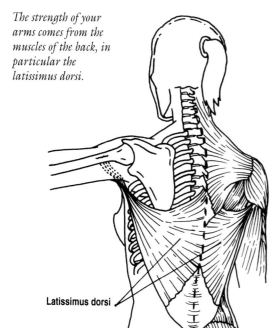

The strength of your arms comes from the muscles of the back, in particular the latissimus dorsi.

Latissimus dorsi

An important set of muscles contributing to the effective use of the arms and assisting in lifting, carrying, pulling and pushing are the two latissimus dorsi muscles (see diagram). With the proper use of the primary control – when the back is lengthening and widening and there is a widening across the shoulders – the arms work as extensions of the back, getting their strength and support from these big back muscles.

The classic misuse, with which we are all too familiar, is to try to get the strength for these activities from the shoulder and arm muscles. Because these are not the correct muscles to use, they will not give you as much strength as you get from using your back muscles. In addition, inappropriate use of these muscles also interferes with the integrated working of the back.

This integrated use of your arms out of the back is also necessary for good use of the hands, and this will make you more sensitive when touching and handling your baby. You may find thinking about your arms extending out of your back and not your shoulders a useful image.

Handling Your Baby

It is always assumed that the mother will know instinctively how to handle a newborn baby, but many women have never held one before, and they feel nervous and tense. If they are in hospital, some women can be intimidated by the health professionals who are the 'experts', and trust themselves even less. However familiar you might be with babies, holding your own is such an emotional experience that you may still feel a little apprehensive. The Alexander Technique can help you in this, teaching you to handle your baby with confidence.

Although your baby can see, hear and smell you, the most important communications he has with you in her early days is through your touch. Babies respond very quickly to the quality of touch. They sense the muscular tension and the movements of their mother. They will sense if they are being held confidently or nervously, with love or with rejection. A baby held in a confident yet gentle and sensitive way will feel more secure and become calm and content. This will make you a very popular baby rocker.

The Alexander Technique also teaches you how to touch sensitively. In the course of having lessons you will notice that the quality of your touch changes. The amount of tension that you have in the whole of your body directly affects the sensitivity that you have in your hands – the less tension, the better the touch. Your ability to sense what it is that you are touching will also be improved.

It is well worth knowing that the baby picks up the parents' use, good use as well as misuse, through her kinaesthetic sense, and learns unconsciously to incorporate this into her own use.

'My Alexander training was invaluable in learning how to "handle" the baby – in the hope that he will develop with good use. It gave me insight into the principle "prevention is better than cure".' *Janet*

Lifting the Alexander Way

New mothers have to spend a great deal of time bending to pick things up
– the baby, toys, changing bags and the paraphernalia associated with
caring for small children – and carrying the same. It is absolutely vital that
you know how to look after your back when you do all these things to
avoid unnecessary strain and injury.

The basis for any bending and lifting action should always be the
monkey or a variation (squat or lunge). Using the ankle, knee and hip
joints for bending ensures that the legs provide a stable base from which to
lower and raise your body to the required height. The further forward the
head goes the further back the hip joints go, and the further forward the
knees go out over the ankles. Using the lever system of your legs and back
means that the work of lifting will be evenly distributed throughout the
body.

If you have been practising the monkey, lunge and squatting during your
pregnancy you will be well equipped to deal with the problems of lifting
once the baby is born.

To pick up the baby from the floor you need to go as close to her as possible. To do this, step forward with one foot and use a lunge to lower yourself into a half-kneeling, half-squatting position; this will give you a stable base, with only the heel of the back foot peeling off the floor. Slide one hand under the baby's head and the other under the back and bottom to give a secure support. As you pick her up, hold her as close to your body as possible, and, using your back and legs as levers, tip your torso over your legs to come up again. Lifting in this way, you can counterbalance the weight of the child in front, by sending your bottom backwards and heels into the ground. Avoid stiffening your neck and remember to direct your back to lengthen and widen. If you are well balanced you will be able to pick the baby up gently and smoothly.

The same principles apply to putting down, because although we are often warned about the dangers of lifting incorrectly, putting something down again can be just as stressful on the back, if not worse.

If you have small children who need picking up, ask them to climb up on to a chair so that you can pick them up from there, rather than having to squat down. This can be made into a game. Instead of lifting them up to your level, which is a strain for your back, sit down with them at their level, either on the floor, or on a small stool. (These ideas are particularly useful if you are pregnant and have small children.)

OTHER POINTS TO NOTE:

• No one area of your body should take the stress of the weight – the strength should come from the whole of your body working as one piece. This may feel strange at first but with practice it becomes the most natural thing to do.

• When lifting an object, do not anticipate how heavy it is just by looking at it. You may tighten your muscles unnecessarily, and this makes the actual lifting harder. It is best to take hold of the object and then let your body gauge how much effort is needed, or if indeed you need to ask for assistance.

• Whatever we have to pick up, from whatever height, we are likely to try to reach for it with our arms before we have lowered our torso near enough. This is an excellent example of end-gaining – trying to reach your goal quickly without thinking about how to get there. You will inevitably have pulled your head back, rounded the back, tightened the legs and lost the connection of the arms into the back. If the object is heavy or precious – and your baby is both – it pays to be especially careful to make sure that the strength of your lifting comes from the whole system with the arms well integrated with the back.

• It may sometimes seem easier not to bother to use your body correctly if an object is small and light. Whatever the weight of the object you are picking up, however, and from however low, it is still important to bend at the hips, knees and ankles and keep the back in one piece. This builds up a habit of using yourself correctly and consciously.

• Wherever possible you should ask someone else to do heavy lifting for you, or divide a big load into smaller parts.

LEFT: *The weight of the baby in this picture is supported by the entire body – no one area is taking the strain.*

RIGHT: *How not to carry your baby! Leaning in this way places a severe stress on the lower back.*

Carrying the Alexander Way

The following are a few tips for maintaining your good use while carrying a lively, kicking baby.

Always carry the baby close to your body. This is better for your back and shoulders and provides love and security for him. If he is facing towards you, you can hold him firmly and securely with one hand under his bottom and the other forearm and hand supporting his back and head.

Babies seem to like being carried to one side against the upper part of the chest, so that they can look over your shoulder. The risk for you is that you may increase your lumbar curve and get backache very quickly. If you adopt a shallow monkey your back will work in one piece and the arms will be freer and stronger to embrace and support your baby. You will also be much more mobile for rocking the baby.

A secure way to hold your baby is to have your arm between her legs and your hand firmly on her bottom.

Carrying the baby with her back towards you is another way of letting her look around at the world. If you place one hand under her bottom and the other hand over the front of her torso she will feel well supported.

Carrying the baby on the hip is so common that it is seen as the right and natural thing to do. In fact, books on child care even suggest this as a good way to carry the slightly older baby, allowing you the use of your free hand. We strongly advise against this practice, however, as it will cause you to twist the spine and hitch one hip up, and can lead to long-term back problems. Even so there will inevitably be times when you cannot put the baby down and you need the other hand to be free. If you do put the baby on your hip be careful not to twist and bend: direct your spine to lengthen and make sure that you are using both legs for support.

The availability of slings and back carriers in which to carry the baby in has given us the advantages women in traditional societies have enjoyed for many years. The baby is held close to the mother's body, either at the front or on the back, which means that neither baby nor mother is anxious about where and how each other is. As well as carrying the baby close to you, you can also have your hands free at the same time, whether at home or out. Jean Liedloff in *The Continuum Concept* argues that a child's sense of security and subsequent ability to be completely independent comes from this early 'in arms' experience.

A baby should not be put into a back carrier before she can support her neck by herself. She should be carried on the front until she gains control of her neck muscles.

When you choose a sling, look for one that gives the best support for the baby's back and head, allowing for the changes in your baby's size, weight and ability to support herself. Also make sure that it feels comfortable for you and is easy to put on and take off. You should be able to wear it with your baby sitting high up and close enough to you, quite snug. If you wear it too loose the baby will hang, putting pressure on your shoulders, causing you to round the upper back and increase the lumbar curve of the spine. If you feel that the baby is not supported properly, you may end up holding her up with your arms, which rather defeats the object of the sling in the first place. A loose sling will give inadequate support to your baby and cause her back to be rounded.

Carrying your baby in a back carrier, once she has control of her neck muscles, encourages you to use your back properly, and to bend using the hips, knees and ankles. If you do not, and you round your back to bend forwards, your precious load will slip up towards your head . . .

Other general points about carrying:
• Try to carry an equal amount with each arm, so that one side is not pulled down.
• Large, heavy loads, and those that don't have handles, should be carried high and close to your body.
• Rucksacks are excellent for shopping and carrying other heavy loads, as your back does the work and your arms are left free.
• Cars are low; whether you are getting in with the baby or putting the baby into the baby seat, hold him as close as possible to your body, and use a monkey or lunge. You will have to incline your head, neck and back a long way forwards from the hip joints to counterbalance your bottom going backwards.

Breastfeeding: The Best Positions

In our modern Western society the skills of holding and positioning breastfeeding babies have to a large extent been lost. Most women now need the help of health workers who can explain how to position the baby properly at the breast. Correct positioning is important because, influenced by images of bottlefeeding with the baby held sideways, women may hold the baby sideways at the breast as well. The baby may learn to suck the nipple instead of taking in the whole areola, and this can lead to soreness and damage in the nipples, as well as closing down milk production (because the necessary triggers for hormonal release are not activated). This is probably one of the most common causes of failure to breastfeed.

Remember that it is possible to bring the baby up to your breast rather than slump down to her. This will also make it easier for her to latch on.

If you are going to breastfeed, to ensure that you and your baby get off to a good start it will help if you feel comfortable and well supported. Many mothers report tension in the neck, shoulders and arms from sitting feeding, and this is of course equally true if you are bottlefeeding. Your attention will naturally be on the baby, and if she is your first you may be so anxious about whether she gets enough milk and is in the right position that you will not have time to think about your own. You may end up putting up with being in an uncomfortable position which then starts to feel normal – the start of misuse. If you cannot find a good supporting position when sitting down to feed, you will be more inclined to tense your neck, hunch your shoulders and grip with your arms. How you use yourself is the primary consideration, and what you will have learned from Alexander lessons before the birth will undoubtedly help.

If you feel sore sitting, always make sure that you have a rubber ring cushion or other soft cushion to sit on. Choose a chair with arms and a high supporting back. You can never have too many cushions and pillows to hand. Use them to raise your arm on the armrest and also to rest the baby on your lap. This will prevent one of the greatest temptations, to lean down over the baby. It is also tempting to cross your legs to raise the baby higher, but this will cause you to twist and strain the back and contract down the front of the torso. Instead, if you are flexible enough, you can lift one leg up and put the foot on the seat. You can also sit on the bed or floor, and lean back against cushions or a settee, with your knees bent.

'Breastfeeding was one of the most obvious stimuli to "pull down" in the front of my body. Supporting a baby even when sitting gives the back plenty of work to do; and as the mother of a new baby tends to be tired for much of the time it is difficult for the back not to collapse to some extent. I found padding out an armchair with plenty of cushions was helpful, but was often surprised at how many cushions were necessary – and the cushions had to be rearranged whenever the baby "changed sides"! In the end I discovered that (for me) lying down next to the baby and feeding him in bed when I was resting was always the most relaxing and least pulling-down position.' *Janet*

We have already looked at how the arms extend out of the back (see page 138). Whether sitting or lying down, make sure you have good support for your back to lengthen and widen. When you hold your baby, allow your arms to lengthen out of your back to cradle her, with her head in the crook of your elbow, and support her back with your forearm and hand. Hold her facing you, belly to belly, and tuck her arm under your arm. With your free hand you can then support your breast and touch her cheek or lower lip with your nipple to stimulate her to find it. Gently squeeze your breast so that the nipple stands straight out and move her closer to you to so that she can latch on. If she does not latch on touch her lip with the nipple again.

It may be that the very best position at the beginning is lying down. Lie on your side and let the baby lie next to you. When your baby is newborn and small, she may need to lie on a pillow to be able to reach your nipple. You may also need extra pillows for support so that you do not strain the muscles under the arm and shoulder that you are lying on, as this can hinder the flow of milk.

Once you have established a comfortable way of feeding the baby and you feel confident about it, you will find that you can do it anywhere and at any time. As the baby learns to hold her head and her back gets stronger she will not need so much support from you.

Feeding your baby lying down can be a very peaceful and restful time for you both.

Nappy-changing

We strongly suggest that if possible when changing your baby you use a high table or surface, so that you do not have to bend down continually. There are many changing trolleys or tables on the market that are designed with this specifically in mind, but you can just as easily use an ordinary table. When you choose one, measure its height against yourself. It should ideally reach to your waist.

Always use the monkey when changing your baby. This, of course, is not a position, but a way to bend the hips, knees and ankles freely while maintaining the length and width of the back. The monkey is a useful position when standing at a fairly high table: you can lean towards the baby and reach for the things you need. Remember to let the back lengthen and at the same time send your hips back and let your knees release slightly forward.

Be careful, too, not to be so intent on the object of your attention – in this case your baby – that you forget to think of your use. You may be leaning towards your baby, talking with her and making eye contact, before you realize that you have poked your chin out, pulled your head back and rounded your back.

Your changing table should ideally reach almost up to your waist, but no higher than your elbows.

Women often find themselves trying to change the baby's nappy in a tiny public toilet or on a bit of floor with barely enough space for the baby, let alone themselves; this is exactly the kind of situation that causes damage to backs. Always make sure that there is space for you to move freely. If you have to perch on your toes when squatting down you will not be balanced; your back will be rounded and tense and the freedom of your arms and hands will be restricted.

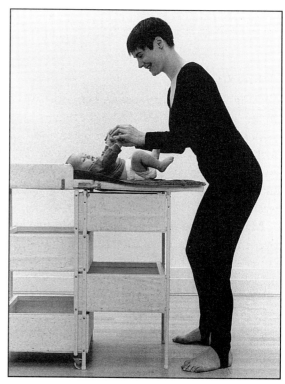

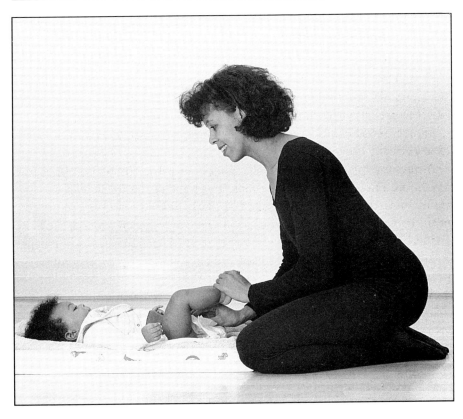

For most people, kneeling is the most comfortable position when changing the baby's nappy on the floor. Whether squatting or kneeling, however, always lengthen your whole head, neck and back forwards freely from the hip joints. You will have much more freedom to lean forwards if you have your knees apart.

Bathing

Bathing your baby can seem much more precarious than most other tasks. If you are not feeling secure and balanced it can easily turn into something both you and your baby dislike. The conventional way to hold the baby is with her head in the crook of your elbow and your hand coming round and holding her upper arm. This way the head and upper back are supported, your hand prevents her slipping, and your other hand is free to wash her.

Many baby baths sit across the bath, making it difficult for you to lean over the bath as well as adequately support your baby. In this situation, either kneel next to the bath or use a low stool so that you can use the principles of the monkey. This will give you a stable back from which you can have free use of your arms.

Ideally you need to be able to bath your baby at elbow height, in a baby bath on a high stand – or in the kitchen sink. You can also quite easily and safely share a bath with her, remembering, of course, to keep the water lukewarm.

Playing

Playing with your baby often entails being on the floor (or quite low down), which can be stressful for your back unless you squat, lunge, kneel or crawl. All these activities keep your back in one piece and allow free movement of the arms. Crawling, for instance, can help some adults correct postural faults, and playing with your baby presents the perfect opportunity to practise without your friends and loved ones (those who do not know about the Alexander Technique) wondering about your sanity! Babies are delighted when you get down and crawl with them.

Pushing the Pram or Pushchair

Again, this is something that you will be doing for some time – perhaps three years – and the baby will become progressively heavier, so the good habits that you acquire at the beginning will pay off in the long run.

It is very important that you are comfortable with the pushchair, and one of the main points to look at is the height. The higher the handles are the easier it will be for you to push. Your partner may be taller than you and if he is also to be able to enjoy taking the baby out this is even more important. However, there is also another aspect to height and that is how high off the ground the baby is. Again we would recommend that you go for as high as possible so that you do not have to bend down low every time you pick the baby up or put her down. It is also nicer for your baby to be on a more sociable level.

To push a pram, simply place your hands on the handle to guide it, and let the impetus for the movement come from your body walking forwards.

The weight of the pushchair is another important consideration. Your baby will soon grow heavy, and you may want to carry shopping on the pushchair as well. You will also have to lift it at some point. Try to test a friend's to get a realistic idea. It is quite a different matter from testing in the shop.

When women push a pram they often use a lot of effort in their arm muscles, which is accompanied by a raising of the shoulders and tensing of the neck. As we have already explained, the power of your arms does not come from your shoulders, but from the muscles of your back. Because a pram is on wheels, all you need to do when you are on a flat surface is to place your hands on the handle to guide the pram and let the impetus for the movement come from your body walking forwards. You do not actually have to push a pram! It is only when you need to push uphill or manoeuvre it up and down pavements and steps and in and out of doorways that you have to use more effort. Again, this should come from the whole of your back rather than from your arms. The higher the handles are the less you are inclined to lean down on to the pram or pushchair. It is this leaning down that makes it seem an effort to push it along. You should also avoid 'gripping' the handles tightly as this will set of a chain reaction of tension up the arms and into the neck and shoulders.

The same applies to pushing supermarket trolleys; this provides a further challenge for maintaining good use in a very demanding situation.

13 | Use and Your Child

There are myriad different factors to be taken into consideration when looking at the development of use in young children. We all come into this world as unique individuals. We interact with a wide range of people and situations and it is impossible to predict what will or will not have an effect on a particular individual. In fact genetic, cultural and psychological influences all play a part, as do the effects of physical environment, diet, childhood illnesses and injuries. Our use can be seen as the psycho-physical expression of a conglomeration of all aspects of life.

Alexander devised a technique that not only gives us the possibility of improving the use of the individual once it has gone wrong, but which also gives us the necessary skills to prevent misuse from developing. In the words of Frank Pierce Jones, an American Alexander teacher, it is a technique for 'learning how to learn'.

The Young Infant

The newborn human baby, unlike other mammals, does not possess immediate muscular control of its body, but will learn all the basic movements during the first two years. Babies learn to sit, crawl, stand, use the hands to manipulate objects, walk, and run in a specific order, capacities that develop with the growth of the central nervous system. Although the rate of development varies, they all go through the same sequence, and the movements involved in each developmental stage are important in developing the neuromuscular skills required for the next. Given a supportive environment, babies will learn these skills on their own, and through a process of trial and error.

The developmental movements that a baby goes through are aimed at creating the right conditions in the musculature and the spine for upright posture. The child basically learns to counteract the force of gravity, gradually refining its balance until it achieves its goal of being upright. First she learns to use her neck muscles so that she can support the weight of her head, then she learns to use her back muscles so that she can sit upright unsupported. Next she learns to crawl, which develops the co-ordination of the arms and legs with the head, neck and back. The baby then repeatedly experiments with coming up from squatting to standing, and going down again. She bends at the hips, knees and ankles and keeps her back in alignment, naturally adopting the Alexander monkey between squatting and upright, at first holding on to something. Through the constant repetition of these movements, she is able eventually to stand unsupported, and goes on to take her first steps. This early learning process develops the proper functioning of the primary control (or head/neck/back relationship) and the anti-gravity mechanisms which enable us to maintain balanced upright posture with ease. In fact postural and muscular co-ordination continues to develop with changes to the skeletal structure, until the age of eight or nine, with a further stage of major changes taking place during puberty.

Even the unskilled eye can recognize the beautiful poise of very young children, and how freely they move without unnecessary tension. If they lose balance, for instance, they do not 'fall', they simply bend at the hips, knees and ankles, and sit down on their bottoms. However, there are factors which influence and interfere with this natural grace, and which can cause faulty muscular tensions and imbalances.

At Their Own Pace

An interesting study of the influences affecting the development of upright posture was carried out in 1938 by one of the first Alexander teachers, Alma Frank. She had become interested in the posture of young children from her observations over a period of years that even nursery-school children showed a deterioration of physical co-ordination. She was curious to know what influences affected upright posture, and which of these were harmful and which helpful.

She compared the neuromuscular co-ordination of babies who were allowed to move from lying on their back to sitting up by themselves, in their own time, with babies who were helped into sitting by being pulled up by their arms. She found that the babies being pulled up by the arms showed the beginnings of the misuse that Alexander had noticed in adults. The arms being pulled upwards caused the head to drop backwards, and the spine to curve and shorten, thus losing the integrity of the head/neck/back relationship and the co-ordination of the limbs into the torso. In contrast, the babies who were allowed to take their own time in sitting up showed the working of the 'primary control' that Alexander had discovered. The baby keeps the spine lengthened, and the head is kept erect and in line with the spine. The arms and legs are free to follow the movement of the head and trunk. There is observably a primary mechanism of co-ordination in operation.

It is imperative to let a baby develop at her own pace. A baby's bones are quite soft and pliable and the purpose of the muscular activity is to mould them into their future shape. (In fact bones have some amount of pliability until the age of sixteen or seventeen.) Forcing a baby to adopt postures and perform movements before the muscular strength and co-ordination is there can cause untold harm to the musculo-skeletal system. In an attempt to support itself, the baby may use the wrong set of muscles for the new activity, and thereby develop muscular imbalances and physically distorted posture. These are the beginnings of misuse. Any imbalance in the baby's body will be corrected by muscular tension to counterbalance it. Both the imbalance and the correction of the imbalance will be incorporated into the baby's movements and form the basis from which all further postural development and learning of movement will take place.

It is extremely important, therefore, that the baby's head is carefully and firmly supported until she has developed proper control of her neck muscles. A baby cannot support her own head in a sitting position before she is about six months old, except for brief moments, even though she has some control of lifting the head while lying down. It is harmful to leave the baby sitting without proper support for any length of time before she can sit upright on her own – on the potty, in high chairs, or on the floor unsupported, for instance. Dr W. Barlow, a medical doctor and Alexander teacher, wrote that many babies will have developed a sideways curvature in their backs by the time they are one year old, a horrifying concept.

Slings or back carriers for transporting a baby must offer proper support for the baby's head and back – some allow the back to be rounded. Putting the baby in a baby walker or door hanging bouncer before she has developed the strength in the back and legs to stand up on her own also encourages twists and curvature of the back and imbalanced use of the legs.

Imitation

'The vast majority of wrong habits acquired by children result from their imitation of the imperfect models confronting them. But how many parents bother to put a right model before their children? How many learn to eradicate their own defects of poise and carriage so that they may be better examples to the child?' *F.M. Alexander*

If you observe a family you will see that as well as physical characteristics there are strong similarities in their use. It seems that upright posture and movement patterns are both hereditary and learned skills. In the early years the predominant way that a child learns is through observation and subconscious imitation of the behaviour of the people around him. Children cannot but learn. They are thirsting to soak up everything that comes their way, and learn through experience and from the examples presented to them. This ability to imitate enables the child to learn the language, habits and manners of his family and culture, but what is less well known is that children also learn about posture and movement through imitation.

A child will mimic manners, posture, movements, facial expressions and breathing. These are all muscular actions, tension patterns which the child will unconsciously learn. Children will copy the parent or carer to whom they are closest, imitating the psychological characteristics and attitudes that are expressed physically in their posture.

If the parents or carers have poor use, this will be picked up by the child. It might be a particular way of walking that throws the whole body out of balance and interferes with the primary control, or a more subtle misuse, for example a faulty pattern of breathing that is a result of an overall misuse. If the parent has had an injury, or has a physical disability, and has developed compensatory tension patterns, the child, although he does not have the same condition, may start to match these muscular patterns in himself. However, good use is not dependent on physical structure and someone with a disability or permanent injury can learn good use just as well as anyone else.

However, if the adult has relatively good use, this sets a better example for the child. If parents have an awareness of their own use they may notice how their children copy them, and this can turn into a learning situation for the adults as well. If, for example, parents notice that their child is pulling his or her head back, they may realize that they are doing it too. From your own learning experiences you will be able to encourage good use in your child.

* * *

The Alexander Technique offers not only a skill for living for the present generation but also a way forward positively to influence our children. Alexander encapsulated his aspirations for future generations when he wrote the following:

'I look for a time when the child shall be so taught and trained that whatever the circumstance which shall later surround it, it will without effort be able to adapt itself to its environment, and be enabled to live its life in the enjoyment of perfect health, physical and mental.'

Beverly (*page 43, top*), 6 months pregnant, had a water birth at home. 'Once the labour started I was just going to relax and give in because I wanted a quick birth. In my head it was going to be short and intense and that's how it was.' Her husband Tony caught baby Dillan and also cut the cord.

Jacqueline (*page 140*), photographed with Matteo, 5 months, had a home birth supported by her partner Paulo, a recently qualified Alexander teacher. 'I spent the whole labour kneeling, and Mateo was born easily, pulling the placenta out with him. He has been a very calm and happy baby.'

Thais (*page 144*) is photographed with son Tom. She had a normal hospital birth and now lives in Brazil, where she is furthering her academic career. 'I'm sure that learning the Alexander Technique was why I felt so fit throughout my pregnancy,' she says, 'and although my labour didn't work out as I had hoped and I wasn't able to use the Technique, I've still found it useful in looking after Tom.'

Michelle (*page 136*) is 6½ months pregnant in the photographs. Despite the fact that Daniel was a very large baby, she had a successful home birth. Two years of Alexander Technique followed by several years practising yoga gives her a body awareness that she finds vital to her life as a mother and a working homeopath.

Gaynor (*page 134*), mother of three, gave birth to Sasha (8 months in photographs) at home. 'It was much better having a home birth, and having Brita's Alexander "hands on" helped me not to tense up and resist. Sasha popped out after only five or six pushing contractions.'

Sophie (*page 43, bottom*), who is 7½ months pregnant in the photographs, had booked for home delivery but because no midwives were available when she went into labour eventually gave birth to Lily in hospital, using only gas and air. 'I did loads of moving and rocking with my hips. In the shower I whistled and sang. The Technique definitely helped.'

Margaret (*page 136*), pictured with 3-month-old Sarah, had a home birth. She is now running a business that manufactures baby slings which hold the baby across the parent's front, allowing the parent's arms and hands to be free – and promoting better use!

Pathika (*page 41, above*), 6 months pregnant, had planned to have her baby at home but because baby Zeno was born prematurely she gave birth in hospital. She lives in Namibia, where she uses the Alexander Technique to, amongst other things, complement the more traditional African sling methods of carrying babies.

Jenny (*page 77*), who was 6 months pregnant in the photographs, had a successful home birth using a birth pool. 'I had to concentrate on staying in the moment all the time – I didn't think about what was coming next . . . ' she says. 'I absolutely love being a mother.'

Jane (*back cover*), a nurse, was 7 months pregnant when she was photographed with her son Tom, 22 months. She gave birth to baby Alice, weighing 9lb 1oz, in hospital. 'It was a so easy that the next day I couldn't have told you that I had just had a baby!'

Rebecca (*front cover*), 5 months pregnant when photographed with 2-year-old Charlie, gave birth to Freya after a 5½-hour labour. 'I had practised squatting throughout pregnancy and gave birth squatting supported by my husband. It was an easy labour, but still very hard work. It was wonderful, I'm planning the next one now!'

Further Reading

Approaching Birth, Sally Inch (Green Print, 1989)
Birth Rights, Sally Inch (Green Print, 1989)
The New Active Birth, Janet Balaskas (Thorsons, 1991)
Water Birth, Janet Balaskas and Yehudi Gordon (Thorsons, 1991)
(Janet Balaskas is the author of many well-known books on childbirth. She introduced the use of yoga to prenatal teaching and has helped to instigate change in maternal practices in many countries over the past decade. The now widely used term 'active birth' was coined by her. She is the founder of the Active Birth Centre (see opposite).
The New Pregnancy and Childbirth, Sheila Kitzinger (Penguin Books, 1989)
The Experience of Childbirth, Sheila Kitzinger (Penguin Books, 1987)
(Sheila Kitzinger is the author of numerous books on childbearing, all of which are excellent and highly recommended.)
Your Body, Your Baby, Your Life, Angela Phillips, Nicky Leap, and Barbara Jacobs (Pandora Press, 1983)
Essential Exercises for the Childbearing Year, Elizabeth Noble (John Murray, 1976)
Birth Without Violence, Frederick Leboyer (Fontana, 1978)
The Voice Book, Michael McCallion (Faber & Faber, 1988)
The Politics of Breastfeeding, Gabrielle Palmer (Pandora Press, 1988)
Shared Parenthood, Johanna Roeber (Century Hutchinson, 1987)

Body Learning: An Introduction to the Alexander Technique, Michael Gelb (Aurum Press, 1981)
Body Know-how: A Practical Guide to the Use of the Alexander Technique in Everyday Life, Jonathan Drake (Thorsons 1991)

The Alexander Principle, Wilfred Barlow (Gollancz, 1990)
The Use of the Self, F. Matthias Alexander (Gollancz, 1985)
The Art of Changing, Glen Park (Ashgrove Press, 1989)
For a comprehensive list of books, published papers, journals and video and audio cassette tapes on the Alexander Technique and related topics, write with an SAE to STAT Books, at the London STAT address.

Useful Addresses
General
ACTIVE BIRTH CENTRE
55 Dartmouth Park Rd, London NW5 1SL
Tel: 071 267 3006
Founded by 'active childbirth' pioneer Janet Balaskas. Offers wide range of workshops, yoga, massage, acupuncture, osteopathy, homeopathy, etc, books and videos. Also hires out birth pools.

CRYSIS
Tel: 071 404 5011
Telephone helpline for parents of babies who are wakeful, demanding and prone to excessive crying.

FORESIGHT (Association for the Promotion of Pre-conceptual Care)
Tel: 0483 427839
Gives advice on securing optimum health and nutritional balance in both parents before conception.

INDEPENDENT MIDWIVES ASSOCIATION
Nightingale Cottage, Shamblehurst Lane, Botley, Hants SO32 2BY
Offers information to enable women to make informed decision about birth. Register of Independent Midwives available on receipt of SAE.

INTERNATIONAL HOME BIRTH
MOVEMENT
41 High Street, Standlake, Oxon OX8 7RH
Provides information packs for pregnant women,
nurses, midwives, etc.

NATIONAL CHILDBIRTH TRUST
Alexandra House, Oldham Terrace, London W3
6NH Tel: 081 992 8637
Offers information and support in pregnancy,
childbirth and early parenthood. Comprehensive
mail order publications list, including books,
cassettes, educational resources and information
leaflets.

OSTEOPATHIC CENTRE FOR CHILDREN
19A Cavendish Square, London W1M 9AD
Tel: 071 495 1231
Cranial osteopathy can be used to locate and
correct disturbances in babies resulting from birth
trauma. The Centre also treats mothers, and has a
nationwide register of paediatric osteopaths.

PARENTS ANONYMOUS
Tel: 071 263 8918
General helpline for parents' worries and
problems.

ASSOCIATION OF RADICAL MIDWIVES
62 Greetby Hill, Ormskirk, Lancs L39 2DT
Tel: 0695 572776
Support group for midwives and mothers.

WELCOME HOME BIRTH PRACTICE
42 Elder Avenue, London N8 8PS
Tel: 081 347 9609
Independent midwives practice for home births.
Alternative therapies and support groups also
available.

SOCIETY OF HOMEOPATHS (has register of
non-medically qualified homeopaths), 2 Artizan
Road, Northampton NN1 4HU Tel: 0604 21400

Alexander Technique addresses

The London address of the Society of Teachers
of the Alexander Technique (STAT) will provide
a list of AT societies around the world (please
send an SAE), and lists of individual teachers can
be obtained from any of these societies.

THE SOCIETY OF TEACHERS OF THE
ALEXANDER TECHNIQUE (STAT)
20 London House, 266 Fulham Rd, London
SW10 9EL

AUSTRALIAN SOCIETY OF TEACHERS OF
THE ALEXANDER TECHNIQUE (AUSTAT)
PO Box 716, Darlinghurst, NSW 2010,
Australia

CANADIAN SOCIETY OF TEACHERS OF
THE ALEXANDER TECHNIQUE
(CANSTAT)
Box 47025, Apt 12, 555 West 12th Avenue,
Vancouver, BC V5Z 3XO, Canada

SOUTH AFRICAN SOCIETY OF TEACHERS
OF THE ALEXANDER TECHNIQUE
(SASTAT)
35 Thornhill Rd, Rondebosch 7700, South
Africa

NORTH AMERICAN SOCIETY OF
TEACHERS OF THE ALEXANDER
TECHNIQUE (NASTAT)
PO Box 5536, Playa del Rey, CA 90296, USA

Index

abdominal muscles, 58, 63
  after birth, 135
  exercises for, 65–6
  in labour, 114, 117, 118, 126
  lax, 64
  in pregnancy, 65
  over-tense, 64
  and use, 64
active labour, 39, 93
adrenalin, 111, 123
Alexander, F. Matthias, 10
Alexander lessons, 30–1
  post-natal, 131
  in pregnancy, 52–3
Alexander procedures, 33–51
Alexander teacher's role at birth, 130
all-fours, 33, 44
  good use, 45
  instructions, 44
  in labour, 44, 90, 104–5
  misuse, 46
  rocking and circling on, 44
antagonistic muscular action, 34
anterior lip, 112
  position for, 113
anti-gravity mechanisms, 153
arms, as extensions of back, 138
  in breastfeeding, 146
  misuse of, 138
  tension in labour, 125
atlanto-occipital joint, 15

baby at birth, 118–19
back, directions for, 26
  tension in labour, 126
backache, 12
  in pregnancy, 82
balance, 16, 17, 55, 67, 152
Barlow, Dr William, 154
bathing baby, 149
Beerbohm Tree, Herbert, 11
Behaviourist school of psychology, 23

birth *see* childbirth and labour
birth canal *see* pelvis
birth support, 128–30
blood pressure, 48, 122
body after birth, 132, 133–7
  in pregnancy, 57
body suit of musculature, 58, 61, 64
Braxton Hicks contractions, 107
breastfeeding, 145–7
  sitting, 146
  lying down, 147
breath-holding, 117, 124
breathing, 12, 17, 19, 74–80
  Alexander and, 74
  in labour, 93, 105–6, 110, 111, 117
  poor habits of, 76, 80
  in pregnancy, 80
  process of, 74, 75
  rhythmicity of, 76
breathlessness, 80

Carpel tunnel syndrome, 87
carriers and slings, 144–5
carrying baby, 143, 144
'centring down', 72
child development, 152–4
childbirth, 34, 88
choice, 24, 29
  in labour and childbirth, 88
  in pregnancy, 56
circulation, 12
comfort, 18
common complaints in pregnancy, 33, 52, 82–7
constipation, 62, 87
constructive conscious control, 23, 29, 89
  in labour, 89
contractions, 120
  (*See also* labour)
co-ordination, 13, 17
crawling, 150, 153
Cripps, Sir Stafford, 11

Dewey, John, 11, 28
diaphragm, 75
direction of use, 23, 25–7
  in labour, 90

directions, 25, 26
directing, process of, 25, 27
  in semi-supine, 50
Drew, Dr Dorothy, 130
dynamic resting, 46–71

end-gaining, 30, 39
  in labour, 91
endorphins, 81, 95, 122–3

face, tension in labour, 124
fainting, 67, 68
fallen arches, 84
father's role at birth, 128–9
fear in labour, 34, 120, 121, 122
feeling *see* sensory awareness
feet, 84
fight or flight response, 122
flexor reflex, 121
Frank, Alma, 153
Freud, Sigmund, 23
functioning *see* use affects functioning

getting out of bed, 70
'going up', 20
good use, 17, 20, 33
  in caring for baby, 138
  in labour, 90
  in pregnancy, 55–6
gravity, force of, 20, 152
  advantage of in childbirth, 94
  effect of, 46, 47

habit, 24
habitual use, 10, 20–1, 24
haemorrhoids, 62, 86
handling baby, 139–55
head, 15
  directions for, 26
head/neck/back relationship *see* primary control
heartburn, 85
hip joints, 59, 69, 83
Huxley, Aldous, 11

imitation, 20, 154–5
inhibition, 23–4
  and direction, 28

in labour, 90
  (*See also* stopping)
intervertebral discs, 26, 47, 75
Irving, Sir Henry, 11

Jones, Frank Pierce, 152

Kegel, Dr Arnold, 60
kinaesthetic sense, 22, 29, 139 (*See also* sensory awareness)
Kitzinger, Sheila, 72
kneeling, 33, 43
  instructions 43
  in labour, 43, 90, 103–4
knees, directions for, 26, 61, 62
knees and legs, tension in labour, 127

labour, 88, 107–19
  birth, 118
  first stage, 108
  onset, 107
  the path the baby takes, 114–15
  second stage, 114–19
  third stage, 119
  transition, 110
Langtry, Lily, 11
latissimus dorsi muscles, 138
lengthening, 64
  in stature, 13, 64
  and widening of back, 26, 138
Liedloff, J., 144
lifting, 71
  baby, 141–2
  good use, 71, 140–2
  poor habits of, 71
  in pregnancy, 71
ligaments, 57, 59
  effect of progesterone, 54, 57, 82, 83, 84
  repair of damage to, 135
lunge, 33, 37
  caring for baby, 140
  instructions, 38
  in labour, 37, 90, 99–100

lying on back, in labour, 93, 94
in pregnancy, 48, 66
lying on side, 72
lying down in semi-supine, 46–51, 70, 71, 134
instructions, 49–50

means whereby, 30
in labour, 91
mind-body, 11
(*See also* psycho-physical unity)
misuse, 9, 12, 18
in pregnancy, 55, 56
monkey, 33, 34
for birth supporter, 96
caring for baby, 140, 148
in daily activities, 35
hands on table, 37
instructions, 36
in labour, 90, 96–8
lifting, 71, 140
mother–baby relationship, 133
mouth, tension in, and pelvic floor, 62, 78, 79
movement, 13, 17–19, 33
in labour, 95
(*See also* active labour *and* positions for labour)
movement sense *see* kinaesthetic sense
muscle tension, 10, 17–19
and pain, 122
common patterns in labour, 123–7
release of unnecessary, 26, 29, 46, 47, 93
muscle tone, 27
healthy, 28, 60, 64, 65, 66

nappy changing, 148–9
neck, directions for, 26
neck muscles, 10, 13, 16
tension in labour, 124
nerve receptors in neck, 16
nervous system, 52, 152
Noble, Elizabeth, 65
'non-doing', 27
non-interference, 23, 89

Odent, Michel, 81
oedema, 87
oxytocin, 123

pain in labour, 34, 81, 105, 120, 121, 122
pelvic floor, 58, 60
after birth, 137
exercises, 62–3
in labour, 61–2, 117, 118
over-tense, 61
in pregnancy, 61–2
problems, 60
and use, 61
pelvis, 59, 85
true pelvis, 59
perineum, 115
placenta, 119
playing with baby, 150
poise, 14
positions for labour, 96–105
first stage, 108
second stage, 116
transition, 111
posterior presentation, 104
posture, 19
primary control, 13–16, 17, 18, 20, 33, 61, 64, 74, 153
FMA's discovery of, 13
physiology of, 15
progesterone, 53, 54, 57, 134
psycho-physical unity, 11, 89
'puffy cheek' breathing, 79, 80, 90, 112, 117
'pulling down', 20
push-chairs and prams, 150–1
pushing urge in labour, 114, 116, 117

reaction, 24
(*See also* stimulus-response)
relaxation 71–2
in labour, 93
rest after birth, 134
resting, 46–51, 71–3
positions 48–51, 71–3

ribcage, 75
ribs, pain in pregnancy, 84
round ligament pain, 85

Sacks, Refia, 79
sacroiliac joints, 59, 82–3
pain in pregnancy, 82
sciatica, 83
self, sense of, 29
after birth, 132–3
(*See also* use *and* psycho-physical unity)
semi-supine position *see* lying down
sensory awareness, 21, 22
improved, 28, 91
unreliable, 21
sensory re-education, 9
Shaw, George Bernard, 11
shoulders, tension in labour, 125
shortening, of back, 13
in stature, 13
show, 108
singing as preparation for labour, 81
'singing who' exercise, 135
sitting, 18
crossing legs, 83, 86
sitting bones, 59
sleeping, 12, 70
in pregnancy, 70
slipped disc, 47
slumping, 18, 54, 83, 84, 85, 87
sounds *see* vocalizing
spine, 13, 14, 47
squatting, 33, 34, 39
caring for baby, 140, 149, 150
counterbalanced, 42
good use, 40
hanging, 41
instructions, 39
in labour, 39, 100–2
in lifting, 140
misuse, 40
supported, 42
standing, 67–8
startle pattern, 121
stimulus-response, 17, 23

stopping, 10, 24
stress, 9, 12
in pregnancy, 52
sub-occipital muscles, 15
supporting baby's head, 141, 144, 149, 154
symphysis pubis, 59, 85
syntometrine, 119,

tension *see* muscle tension
thinking, 9, 17, 19
thinking in activity, 28
thinking into body, 25, 27, 92
Tinbergen, Prof. Nikolaas, 11
touch, 139
transition *see* labour

unreliable sensory awareness, 21
upright labour, advantages of, 93–6
upright posture, 13, 18, 19, 153
use affects functioning, 12
use, of the self, 12
after birth, 134
in labour, 89
in pregnancy, 52–4
uterus, 58–9

varicose veins, 62, 86
visualization, 92
vocalizing in pregnancy, 80–1
in labour, 90, 106

walking, 69–70
water retention *see* oedema
waters breaking, 108
weight increase in pregnancy, 54
'whispered ah', 76–8, 80, 81
in labour, 90, 112, 117
and pelvic floor release, 78
widening, back, 26